I THINK, THEREFORE I ASK

Other books by Mukunda Rao

Fiction

Confessions of a Sanyasi (1988)

The Mahatma: A Novel (1992)

The Death of an Activist (1997)

Chinnamani's World (2003, 2025)

In Search of Shiva (2010)

Shambuka Rama: Three Tales Retold (2018)

Non-fiction

Babasaheb Ambedkar: Trials with Truth (2000)

The Other Side of Belief: Interpreting U.G. Krishnamurti (2005)

The Penguin U.G. Krishnamurti Reader (Ed.) (2007)

The Biology of Enlightenment: Unpublished Early Conversation of U.G. Krishnamurti After He Came into the Natural State (1967–71) (Ed.) (2011)

Between the Serpent and the Rope: Ashrams, Traditions, Avatars, Sages and Con Artists (2014)

The Buddha: An Alternative Narrative of His Life and Teaching (2017)

Sky-clad: The Extraordinary Life and Times of Akka Mahadevi (2018)

MUKUNDA RAO

I THINK, THEREFORE I ASK

A HANDBOOK FOR INTELLIGENT LIVING

Published by Westland Books, a division of Nasadiya Technologies Private Limited, in 2025

No. 269/2B, First Floor, 'Irai Arul', Vimalraj Street, Nethaji Nagar, Alapakkam Main Road, Maduravoyal, Chennai 600095

Westland and the Westland logo are the trademarks of Nasadiya Technologies Private Limited, or its affiliates.

ISBN: 9788198878588

10 9 8 7 6 5 4 3 2 1

Typeset by Mukul

Printed at Thomson Press (India) Ltd

To Vivek Phadnis and Dr Mundra,
with fond memories

Contents

Preface

EVERYONE IS A PHILOSOPHER IN A SENSE. EVERYONE is a conscious subject, thinking and feeling in images and ideas. Animals, it would appear, do not think and live as humans do; rather, they possess an intelligence of their own. Increasingly, there's scientific evidence that animals have much more complex internal lives than was previously thought. Humans possess an animal instinct too, only it is overlaid by thought and thought rules our lives.

We do not know when this thinking–feeling subject—the self-conscious, self-reflexive human—came into being; when ideas arose and the play of life began. Of course, there are several scientific theories about how we evolved alongside several myths offering metaphorical narratives about the origins and development of not only self-conscious human beings but also other life forms and the universe. Related to these myths are beliefs or ideas about gods, souls, life after death, the meaning and purpose of existence and so on. Almost every culture in the world has held such ideas over centuries, shaping human thinking and living—ideas such as a god created the world, the mortality of the body and the immortality of the soul, and the notion of life beyond death are concepts that we absorb from various cultures across space and time.

So, when we issue statements such as god is the creator or that we suffer because of the original sin or that desire is the cause of sorrow or that our karma is what decides our fate, we are actually picking out ideas from the pools of human thought we have created over thousands of years. Even what we call moral or common sense that is considered to be sound, practical judgement of everyday matters is not something that is natural or innate. We have absorbed these ideas after years of ideological conditioning and they have now become a part of us.

In other words, for centuries now, people have asked questions about the existence of god, the meaning and purpose of life, if we have souls, if we have free will, if our lives are predetermined, about love, freedom, nature and so on. And they have come up with numerous answers from various perspectives—lived experiences, religion, science or the arts. Today, there are plenty of answers to almost every question.

Yet, doubts and problems persist. We are, of course, not talking of technical questions, or those related to the physical or material side of our lives. We are concerned with the dilemmas we face in the psychological and social realms—issues related to interpersonal relationships, questions about god, the purpose of life, fears and anxieties, love and hatred, loneliness and death.

It's still unclear if the beliefs and ideals we have been trying to follow are conducive to intelligent, harmonious and happy living. But our mind is full of desires that drive us in different directions. Along with feelings of jealousy and anxiety, this troubles us to no end. People are not merely flesh and bone. Their beliefs are what set them apart. And when you talk with them about sensitive issues, such as relationships, god or politics, you realise how little you really understand people—including your near and dear ones—and how little you know yourself. That is when questions like 'Where did my beliefs come from? Who are these people? What am I? What is this life?' pop up in your mind.

You want to know; you need some clarity to move on, at least a functional clarity if not an enduring certainty. Would a steadfast political revolution or an assiduous religious jihad end all your troubles? Would belief in and prayers to god calm your restless mind and relieve you of doubts and anxieties? Could love or a little more money be the solution? These are questions you ask yourself and others as well. You listen to the discourses of gurus or search for answers in texts written by theologians, philosophers and political thinkers.

But, as stated earlier, the fact is that you already know a lot. You are a thinking, feeling animal walking on two legs, with opinions on diverse subjects ranging from sex to corruption. All you need to do is to see the relentless movement of life for beliefs and emotions to well up and start brewing within you.

Whether you know it or not, all sorts of ideas and beliefs pervade your being. That is why there is no such thing as starting afresh. Instead, there is only the possibility of critically examining and understanding what is already present, and then perhaps following your inner voice and going with the flow without getting swept away by any particular idea. In other words, we cannot go back and start from the beginning; we can start only from where we are today. All we can do is question the answers that have already been given, and see if they make sense to us and enhance our life.

One must accept that a neutral perspective doesn't exist either. On deeper analysis, you realise that there is an opinion behind every idea or philosophy. When we say something is evil, or that somebody is good, we are most likely expressing a point of view formed under the influence of some belief system, rather than our experience of reality.

There are no absolutes in life. Hence, no answer can be considered conclusive. All concepts and philosophies are relative, including the ones in this book, because they possess only a relative and functional value, not an absolute one. Therefore, this critical inquiry is going to be double-edged; a fun yet illuminating undertaking, challenging the binarising and absolutising tendency of traditional discourses.

If philosophy is the pursuit of wisdom or love of wisdom, then it has to be critical, unpretentious, honest and open-ended. It cannot be another ism, or a theory to refute other theories. Instead, it ought to interrogate why all our beliefs and ideas, including those that come under religious and political faith, are part of a conditioning process that has, over the centuries, moulded human behaviour—good, bad and ugly.

I Think, Therefore I Ask is an invitation to readers to open themselves to the varied views of life and to the radical understanding that these are all only views constructed over centuries that often reflect belief systems, none of which can be equated with truth. Through this book, I ask readers to doubt, to question and to break free from all prejudices and conclusions.

Truth is something we do not know—that perhaps is the only truth if there is one: that we do not know. Nobody does, not even great thinkers, visionaries, politicians, scientists and gurus. More often than not, political leaders and religious gurus, who preach and make decisions that impact our lives, have little understanding of the consequences of their words and actions. Like the rest of us, they too are subject to fear, desire, prejudice and anxiety, and have needs for love, recognition and security. Like everyone else, they also eat to live, sleep, dream, suffer and die one day.

It seems life has its own logic, its own play at work, which surprises us at every turn. It bemuses us and teaches us about the mysteries of existence. Sometimes, it may express itself as our inner voice, as the gurgling laughter of a child, as the blooming of a flower or the falling of yellow leaves from trees. But often, caught in the pressures of everyday living, we do not see or hear what life is trying to tell us. We know that life is not going according to our plan, but we are not ready to accept that. We live in denial, disconnected from the flow of things.

Let me put it another way. All history is a past upon which we have *inscribed* a structure of meaning and constructed elaborate stories: yours, mine and that of humanity at large. We live and move within these stories while always wondering if there is a higher truth beyond them. And if that higher truth does exist, can we capture it within the framework of a particular philosophy? That seems impossible, given the divisive nature of our perception of life. Yet it is a paradox that the thought–feeling (which is a unitary movement not outside of nature but within the ebb and flow of life) is all we have to quest after truth, to know ourselves, to play, argue and fight with, or nourish life. It is not a tragedy, or an existential angst, or a cause for despair. It is a terrific enigma.

We are born of the womb of our mothers. We grow up, learn to speak and construct our own little stories based on what we have learnt over the years. We build bonds based on love, loyalty, distrust and hate. We create structures of belief and order, rebel against them when we find them to be oppressive and violent and yearn for freedom. There is joy in all these endeavours, as well as conflict and sorrow. We are intelligent, but also stupid. We live paradoxically.

How we use our emotions depends entirely on us. We can use them to break free from constraints and live intelligently, or drag ourselves down through a morass of conflict and suffering. To be true to ourselves, to listen to our inner voice needs no time. It can begin now, provided we take the journey with an open mind and not arrive at any hard conclusions. It is crucial to be honest with ourselves, to let whatever is discussed here unfold and reveal itself for what it is in the context of our day-to-day living.

The world of philosophical ideas is an inexhaustible one. Even if we succeed in making a nearly complete inventory, it would be impossible to critically examine them all, and it is certainly not within the scope of this text. So, this little book has to be seen as an introductory work, a primer of sorts.

When I first started writing it, I had in mind the youngsters of today as my audience. To me, they seem less inhibited, more confident; free from the problems that the older generation faces. But I also find them terribly confused, often subject to anxiety and panic when it comes to living in a rapidly changing world. They needed a book that would bring to the table the many ideas and beliefs in their lives and explain things in a simpler, accessible language so that they can make the right decisions. But soon I realised that the adults are in a far worse situation than the youngsters. Incarcerated in their beliefs, they have stopped asking questions; rather, they stubbornly continue to cling to the many unexamined notions that have made a mess of their lives and deserve to be discarded. They need to travel light during their last stretch before they leave to make room for the younger generations.

That is how this book grew, like a peepal tree with many branches, to include readers of all ages and from all backgrounds. I hope, therefore, that this book is accessible to all kinds of people. I trust that the effort will not have been in vain if it encourages them to question and critically examine not only the beliefs that surround them but also their own, in order to live wisely.

I'm deeply indebted to the various authors and their books from where I have drawn inspiration. More importantly, in a sense, this book marks a crystallisation of some of the central themes I have addressed in my previous work, and I must confess that I have borrowed freely from them. Lastly, in a book of this nature, repetition of certain ideas and expressions is inevitable, and it is my hope that the reader will understand that reiteration is quite necessary in order to highlight the issues I'm addressing.

I
Life

ONE SUMMER NIGHT, WHEN THE STARS WERE OUT and a pleasant breeze swept across the land, Bahurupi, the one with many faces, a teller of stories, clad in a long ochre robe and an orange turban, appeared on a stage that had been lit up by the flares of burning torches. He thundered:

'Friends, the idea of the beginning is an illusion, since every beginning is already a second one, a third one, a hundredth one. It's a terrific cycle, never ending. You know, everything is a story within a story, like a circle within a circle. There are only stories, yours, mine and of the Great Unknown that is everywhere and in everything, like salt in the sea.'

Bahurupi is surely a clever storyteller, but what he says rings a bell, doesn't it? For who knows if the idea of origin could be a trick of the mind? That our lives could be like stories within stories and without a beginning? Even if we assume that there is such a thing as the beginning or origin of life, will it be possible to know that through our binary mind? And will the mind, which is an integral part of the very life it wants to look into, know its own beginning?

There are numerous theories and myths about the origins of life. We do not know if they are true. But they are all interesting, educated speculations that have influenced our thinking. I have examined some of them here to see where they lead us.

Let us take up some of the major scientific theories first. It is said that life originated on earth from what they call the primordial soup, that is, a mixture of molecules that were created following a set of favourable conditions around four billion years ago in the ocean, within warm, rocky nooks called deep sea vents. In terms of the origin of earth and the universe itself, the Big Bang theory is perhaps the most accepted one. It is believed that some 13.8 billion years ago, the universe was born in a big bang. What was originally a little thing, like a grain of sand or atom, became terribly hot, exploded and began to expand. Scientists believe that the universe is still growing. Eventually, as the heat abated, all the elements cooled enough, leading to the formation of the universe with all its stars, planets and galaxies, and then, finally, the birth of life on earth. However, given the ongoing explorations in physics, especially in the field of astronomy, it has its doubters.

There are other theories as well, such as the RNA world, electric spark and extraterrestrial origin. According to the extraterrestrial origin theory, life was formed not on our planet but somewhere else in deep space, or on a distant planet, and then these life forms were carried to earth by meteorites or extraterrestrials.

In effect, all these theories suggest that earth and life were created not by some god, or a supernatural, external power, but by unknown natural causes. Then, over a long period of time, simple cells evolved into complex structures of life.

In contrast to the many scientific theories of creation, there are many lively myths of creation across cultures. It is not possible to recount them all here. However, it is interesting to note that terms such as beginning, void, nothing, darkness, water, light, word, unity, separation recur in several of these stories, for instance, in Māori and Uitoto cosmogony and in Zoroastrian, African, Mayan, Egyptian, Japanese, Chinese, Mesopotamian and Indian mythical tales of creation.

These mythical tales carry three major themes:

- A higher being created the universe and life, including human beings, by thought, word or heat. But this god or power is outside of the creation of the supreme being.
- A primordial being, primeval entity or cosmogenic egg split itself in two and became all creation.
- In the beginning, all was one, a kind of humongous, amorphous mass. And creation involved splitting up the primordial mass in two. Hence, heaven and earth, male and female, life and death.

In all the major religions of the world, these stories of creation primarily revolve around three different conceptions of god.

- The primordial power, generally referred to as god, is outside of creation;
- God is transcendental; and

- God is immanent, that is, god is in the universe and the universe is in god.

It is critical to note that these creation myths, while metaphorical (though hardcore believers may take them literally), have served as philosophies of life. Within these frameworks, theologians and philosophers over centuries have constructed concepts of man, woman, their relationship to nature, to god, and the meaning and purpose of life. All these ideas have influenced people tremendously. Keeping this in mind, let us consider two major stories of creation, namely, the story of creation according to the Bible and the myth of Prajapati from Brihadaranyaka Upanishad.

Genesis

> In the beginning God created the heaven and the earth. And the earth was without form, and void; and darkness was upon the face of the deep. And the Spirit of God moved upon the face of the waters. And God said, let there be light: and there was light. And God saw that the light was good; and God separated the light from the darkness. God called the light Day, and the darkness he called Night. And there was evening and there was morning, the first day.

This way, over six days, the Bible says that a god created the sky, the land, plants, the sun and moon and all creatures, including 'human kind in our image, according to our likeness; and let them have dominion over the fish of the sea, and over the birds of the air and over the cattle, and over all the wild animals of the earth, and over every creeping thing that creeps upon the earth.'

In the second story of the Genesis, god created the first man, Adam, from the earth. He made a garden in Eden for Adam. But when he saw that Adam was lonely, he took one of his ribs and created a companion for him, the first woman, Eve. God then forbade them to eat fruit from the 'tree of the knowledge of good and evil'.

Adam and Eve lived in paradise, in joy, in complete innocence, until the day a serpent, an element of the devil or Satan himself, enticed them to eat the forbidden fruit from the tree of the knowledge. As punishment for their disobedience, god banished the couple from the Garden of Eden. Consequently, the primordial pair, from whom humanity emerged, lost their innocence and their unity of being.

In the Christian world, the eating of the fruit of knowledge is seen as the fall of man, the 'original sin' that ruined god's plan. That is why the descendants of the ancient couple are forced to live a life of hardship, caught in the struggle between the forces of good and evil. They also believe that the sorrow can be ended if humans repent for the sins committed by Adam and Eve and surrender to the will of god. On the other hand, certain sects within the Christian world have interpreted the fall of man not as a sin that needs expiation but as an opportunity to learn the difference between good and evil, and side with good, hoping and praying for salvation.

The Myth of Prajapathi

The Rigveda (10.121) depicts Hiranyagarbha, the 'golden womb', as the source of the creation of the universe. In the same text, in the 'Purusha Sukta' (10.90), there is also the idea of the cosmic being, Purusha, who is sacrificed by the gods. The universe is then created using different parts of Purusha's body, almost similar to the cosmic egg motif found in the creation stories of other cultures. However, it was in the Brihadaranyaka Upanishad that the creation myth was fully and brilliantly developed. Here is the edited version:

> In the beginning, this universe was nothing but It, the Self in the form of a person. It looked around and saw that there was nothing but itself, whereupon its first shout was, 'It is I!'. This is where the concept 'I' arose. (And i.e. why, even now, when addressed, one answers first 'It is I!', only then giving the other name that one bears.)
>
> Then it was afraid because it is alone. But it thought: 'Since there is no one here but myself, what is there to fear?', whereupon the fear departed.
>
> However, it still lacked delight (which is why we lack delight when we are alone) and desired a second. The person was exactly as large as a man and woman embracing. This Self then divided itself into two parts. And from that man and woman came into being.
>
> The male embraced the female, and the human race took birth. She, however, reflected: 'How can he unite with me, who is produced from himself? Well, then, let me hide!' She became a cow, he a bull and united with her. And from those cattle arose. She became a mare; he a stallion. She an ass; he a donkey. Solid-hoofed animals arose from that. This continued down to the ants. Then he realised, 'I, actually, am creation; for I have poured forth all this.' Hence, he became known as creation.

Variations of this primary myth of god or the primordial being splitting itself into male and female and becoming all creation can be found in many ancient cultures. How this myth developed into monotheism—into a transcendent male god in some cultures and as an eternal principle embedded in all creation in some others—would make a fascinating story.

That said, what the Prajapathi myth probably indicates is that what had been one became two, hence man and woman, life and death. In other words, the split in consciousness was the beginning of an ego-self. This was transformed into an acute sense of separateness, which in turn led to tremendous dissatisfaction. Efforts were then made to escape from a desolate state of mind by seeking an anchor in life. This flux of emotions also triggered the yearning to return to the state of unitary consciousness.

In a similar vein, instead of taking the fall as depicted in Genesis literally, perhaps it is possible to interpret Adam's 'original sin' not as an unalterable wrongdoing but simply as ignorance of our oneness—that there is no two. In other words, the sin may be seen as a brilliant metaphor to suggest the split in the primordial unitary consciousness, the birth of 'I', loss of innocence, the beginning of the self-conscious, self-reflexive adventure of the human and the struggle to return to the state of the unity of being.

All theories of creation, according to science, remain undecided. However, the search continues. Scientists are looking at quantum theory, quarks, dark matter and dark energy to explain the origin of the universe which is predominantly composed of dark energy and dark matter. Visible matter only makes up around 15 per cent of the universe. Scientists are investigating the nature of the unknown 85 per cent.

In December 2021, the James Webb Space Telescope (JWST) was launched into deep space to study and send back information about planets, galaxies, stars and cosmic objects. It is said that the JWST is several times more advanced than the Hubble Space Telescope and that this massive eye in outer space is looking at the universe like never before. The stunning pictures it has taken has led to the discovery of thousands of new galaxies more distant and ancient than the ones previously known to mankind. Whether these photographs confirm the Big Bang theory is something we will have to wait and see. However, it is believed that we may be on the cusp of information that may compel us to radically review the hitherto accepted physical laws of the universe.

There is no doubt that we know a lot about the universe and life, but it remains limited compared with what we do not. This knowledge, however, has not made us humble. Nevertheless, there are some people of science who are more open-minded than religious ones about how humans came into being.

Myths about creation are all stories—attempts made by previous generations to make sense of the universe and life. They talk to us in metaphors about the mystery of creation; about human desire; the longing for meaning, happiness, peace, power and immortality. 'Myth is poetry,' said Joseph Campbell, a famous mythologist. 'It is metaphorical, and the penultimate truth because the ultimate cannot be put in words.' In other words, myths indicate a thought process that cannot be pitched against reason and science.

There is a need to distinguish between good myths and bad myths. Good myths are those that have a liberating effect and open up new ways of seeing life and the world. Bad myths are those that are chauvinistic and oppressive, producing irreconcilable conflicts and minimising our ability to understand life. Any effort to squeeze emancipatory meaning out of the bad myths is not going to help. It is better to confine them to the pages of history and move on.

So, What is Life?

As I have mentioned so far, we actually do not know the origin of life, despite the many theories that surround it. In effect, the theories about dark energy and dark matter are surely an admission of the fact that what we know is precious little. Everything human beings have experienced, thought and felt since we began to walk on two legs (around two or three million years ago, according to evolutionists), is embedded in the human structure and has shaped consciousness. Yet, we cannot claim to know all about human life—the body, mind and spirit—let alone the totality of it. Despite our vast knowledge, life remains an enigma.

Flux is another word for life. It implies continuous flow, ever-changing, and cannot be captured within the fishbowl of thought, for it will be like attempting to fix a point in a stream. Greek philosopher Heraclitus is believed to have said, 'You cannot step into the same stream twice,' to which one of his disciples responded, 'You cannot step into the same stream even once.'

This means that we cannot claim to know even the dynamic present, for our mind, given its nature to think in pairs of opposites and in a linear fashion, cannot perceive it. In other words, we use knowledge to perceive the present, even though knowledge is based on memory, which means it belongs to the past.

Life expresses itself in boundless ways, some of which we seem to understand, but most of which we don't. Just as the animals, birds, flowers, mountains, rivers and the innumerable galaxies are expressions of life, self-conscious, self-reflexive humans are also another expression of it.

The Difference between Life and Living

It is imperative to distinguish between life and living, though we often use both words as synonyms. What we call life, phenomena or existence are all deeply philosophical concepts. It bears reiterating that we do not know the totality of life. If our mind cannot capture the flow of life in its entirety, how can we understand its origin? Therefore, when we talk of living, we are actually thinking about our day-to-day existence, our fears and anxieties, our joys and sorrows, our religions and politics. Life, on the other hand, is complex, vast and infinite—it is our idea of it that has an impact on our everyday living.

Is There Any Meaning and Purpose to Our Living?

Living is a challenge for humans. Animals don't face the issues we do. They just live by instinct according to their unique nature and pass away when the time comes. When hungry, a tiger doesn't ask itself whether it should kill or not. It does what's required and, once satiated, may lie down in the shade of a tree and doze off. Let a monkey into the plantain grove and it will pluck and eat some ripe bananas. In the process, it may destroy many unripe fruit but that is of no concern to the primate.

Only human beings ask questions about the meaning and purpose of existence. We do so because we have an urge to know and find a possible solution to our problems. We are also motivated by the fact that other people are looking for the same answers, and hence it seems natural and important. We ask questions when there is suffering, when we are in pain, when we see death. But in moments of excitement and joy, these questions disappear.

But is there really any meaning and purpose to our existence? The many belief systems of the world are all attempts to answer this question. They are complex and persuasive; contradictory and dogmatic, too. But have these answers enabled people to live intelligent and happy lives, in harmony with nature and the world?

Let's take a few more questions: Are women equal to men? Are those who identify as LGBTQ+ abnormal, an aberration or are they natural and as much children of the universe as others? Are all religions equal, or are some paths to god/truth/reality superior to others? There are thousands of religious, spiritual and philosophical texts, so why do some believe that their scripture alone is the text inspired by god and has answers to all questions about life? Is god male or female, or neither? How does one talk about god, if there even is one? Is god omniscient and merciful; if so, how can such a god reward and punish people? If god is perfect and all-powerful, why did such an entity create an imperfect world prone to earthquakes, hurricanes, tornadoes and droughts that destroy life and property, and create such human beings who are susceptible to disease, jealousy, hate and violence?

Would answers to these questions give a sense of direction to our lives, offer meaning and purpose to our existence? The truth is that we are tired of constantly trying to adjust our lives according to the answers proffered by society. Trying to live up to our beliefs and values has exhausted us. And the anxieties and pressures we experience in relationships have only made it worse. Failures and disappointments, frustration and suffering, fear of losing what we have or not getting what we desire have all left us weary. We are tired of the whole business of living, and we wonder if this is all there is to life.

Once, an eighty-year-old gentleman, a writer of many spiritual books, went to see a sage. He asked the wise man, 'What is the meaning of life? I have written many popular books about the meaning and purpose of life, and tried to interpret the scriptures. But I must confess that I have not understood the meaning of life and I can't stop wondering about why I exist. You are an enlightened one. I hope you'll be kind enough to put my questions to rest.'

The sage said, 'You are eighty years old and you say you have not understood the meaning of life. Why then did you write books on the subject? When are you going to understand that there may not be any meaning to life at all? Tell me, why should life have any meaning? Why should there be any purpose to living? Living itself is all that is there, isn't it? Surely there is a reason for you to come here; a reason why you go for a walk in the morning; why you went to college, earned a degree, took a job, got married and decided to have children. That is what everyone did and you followed their example. But the problem is you are looking for some greater meaning and grander purpose to why you are on earth, which just doesn't exist. And that is a depressing thought. What if you forget about this whole business of meaning and purpose. What happens then? Have you thought about it?'

'Is it possible to drop this search? What am I left with then?' the old man asked.

'What is left? Life and living,' said the sage and laughed. 'Now, listen. You do not feel connected to the totality of life. But are you really detached from life, from the world? What if it is all connected and you just don't perceive it that way? It is this gulf that has created an illusion of the self in us. It has led us to believe that we are special, that we are born with a grander purpose when compared with other species. We think that human beings are immortal, who survive the cycle of death and continue as a soul. Do we know if that is true, or is it just an idea we have constructed through our imagination?'

The old man nodded.

The sage continued. 'It must have been clear to you by now that your quest for meaning and purpose for living has created problems. It's time to let go of this futile search. Give back all that you took from books and society. Return all the ideas, beliefs and dreams, religion and politics. Breathe freely, eat when you are hungry and rest when tired. Look at how life goes on, how it doesn't wait for you or move according to your petty ideas and beliefs in gods and goals. On your way here, did you see the dark clouds in the sky? The monsoon is here. Go home, sit on the veranda or step out of the house and feel the breeze on your face. Watch how the rain transforms the landscape around you.'

God-centric Views

All major religions, with the exception of Jainism, Buddhism and Taoism, derive the meaning and significance of life from their conception of god. All their ideas about the origins of life; purpose of human existence; notions of reward, punishment, heaven, hell and the afterlife are related to a belief in god.

In Judaism, the emphasis is not so much on salvation according to god's plan as it is in seeking justice, compassion and peace that would take believers closer to god, in harmony with his covenant. This material world is god's revelation and within this physical realm, humans shall give life to the soul.

Broadly speaking, the sole purpose of human existence, according to the different sects within Christianity, namely, Catholic, Protestants, Eastern Orthodox, Anglican and so on, is to seek god and surrender to him. They believe that alone gives meaning to human living—reaching their full potential and returning to live with god, not on earth but in heaven. In Islam too, the ultimate purpose of human existence is to revere and worship god, Allah, including his revelations and messengers, strictly follow his instructions as given in the scripture and be unfailingly grateful to him through love and devotion.

Many sects of Hinduism believe in gods and goddesses, considered the elemental and creative forces of the universe, and believe that without their help, it is not possible to negotiate the problems of living. Here, the human condition is likened to the wheels of a cart, which can move smoothly towards the destination of happiness only when they are oiled through belief in, prayer to and protection of deities. Then there are non-dual traditions within Hinduism that are not entirely antithetical to the belief in god, prayers and ritual, but emphasise contemplation on the nature of reality. The concepts of Atman and Brahman are central to these traditions. Atman is not the ego but the essential being of all life forms, human in particular. Brahman is the infinite, immanent, transcendent reality. It is the ground and source of all matter, energy, time, space, being, and everything of and beyond this visible world. To realise this truth—that Brahman is the ultimate reality, that Atman is the same as Brahman—is considered the highest state of being and the final meaning and goal of life.

Purusharthas are the four successive goals of life and may be seen as a creative compromise between the worldly and the non-worldly. They are part of a practical approach to an intelligent way of living. The goals are: artha (producing and enjoying wealth and prosperity), kama (desire, love and sensual pleasure), dharma (righteousness, duty and ethics) and moksha (ultimate liberation from attachment, from the continuity of samsara or self).

Non-theistic Religions

In Jainism, there is no idea of god as the all-knowing, transcendental creator. It proposes that the universe is independent and eternal with different lokas, realms of existence. The supreme reality or knowledge, kaivalya, rules life. The attainment of kaivalya—freedom from karmic bonds, or release from the cycles of birth and death—is the ultimate goal of life. The belief and practice of ahimsa in thought, word and deed is also an integral part of the religion.

Taoism, also known as Daoism, is a set of Chinese traditions and spiritual movements that goes back to the fourth century BCE. Dao means the way or path, and is also described, like Brahman in Advaita Vedanta, as the principle underlying reality. You do not worship Dao, like you do a god in monotheistic religions. Rather you grow and live in harmony with Dao. Compassion, simplicity, spontaneity and humility are its guiding values.

Buddhism, too, has no god, but it is not an atheistic religion as many Western scholars have called it. The aim of life here is twofold: to overcome sorrow, which includes all forms of suffering, or beliefs and practices that produce conflict and suffering, and to attain nirvana, a state of being where there is no sadness or discord and one is established in the blissful awareness of the unity of all life.

Non-religious Meaning and Purpose of Life

There are many non-religious expressions of human potential and ideals that may sound like adages today. While they may seem like wisdom distilled from the lived experiences of people over centuries, these expressions can also be understood as ideas gleaned from philosophers like Charvaka, Confucius, Socrates and Sartre.

- It is good to dream and strive to realise one's dream, for that is what gives meaning and direction to our lives.
- We need to stand up for ideals and values that enhance the purpose of our existence.
- It is absurd to look for meaning when there is none. However, it is possible to create it for one's own life and live for it. Therein lies the significance of life.
- The meaning we give to life is subjective. You nurture the reason that is true to you and follow it as best as you can.
- There is real value in being authentic in thought, deed and action.
- Live for others and to work towards the greater good of humanity.

- Love alone gives meaning to life.
- There is no world other than this—no heaven and no hell. The idea of god is an invention. To have fun and enjoy life to the fullest extent is possible. Just learn to live joyously.
- God is dead, and looking for meaning is a futile exercise. Everything is accidental; therefore, we need to make the best of our situation and live as fully as possible.
- Humans are thinking and talking animals, given to aggression. The sooner we accept this fact, the better it is for humanity.
- It is possible to create a society based on egalitarian values and the ethics of non-violence. That is how we develop democratic spaces, where each individual has the opportunity to actualise their potential, and grow into a healthy, intelligent and compassionate human being.

History as an Unfoldment of Meaning and Purpose

Indian enlightenment traditions have to be distinguished from the European Enlightenment movement that developed and spread between the late seventeenth and the early nineteenth centuries.

The former, starting from the Upanishadic times to the modern period, laid emphasis on the possibility of individuals stepping off the river of samsara enmeshed in divisive values and conflicts, while pursuing illusory gods and goals to live an unfettered life. The European Enlightenment movements, influenced by the ideas of John Locke, Thomas Hobbes, Jean-Jacques Rousseau, Adam Smith, Immanuel Kant, Karl Marx and other thinkers, prioritised reason, skepticism, secularism, individualism and political activism to usher in a society rooted in liberty, progress, toleration, fraternity and separation of constitutional governments from religions.

For the thinkers of the European Enlightenment tradition, notions of meaning and purpose of life were embedded in the idea of (goal-oriented) history. Marxists constructed an elaborate pattern of history that would inevitably lead to the collapse of old ideas and (capitalist) patterns of living, ushering in revolutionary changes in society for greater good.

History, as an ethical guide and story of progress, reason and justice, replaced an omniscient, omnipotent and omnipresent god. Religious beliefs in god and his covenant and the idea of salvation of humanity were substituted by notions of development, progress and the eventual deliverance of humanity from poverty, injustice and suffering.

Now, what do these numerous catalogued views on the meaning and purpose of life tell us? Which view is correct? Is there such a thing as the right view? Can all views be correct or wrong? Or is each view correct from its own perspective?

A Hindu may not agree with the Muslim view of life; a Marxist may find the Christian view of life irrational and regressive. A Christian may find the godless world of the Marxists blasphemous and wish for its elimination from the world. One who thinks of himself as modern and scientific may find tribal life primitive and barbarous, while tribal people may consider modern men ignorant, immature and heartless.

While there may be some truth in all views, can we equate any particular view with truth? In our quest for answers to questions on god, the meaning of life, suffering and evil, death and the afterlife, we have constructed many belief systems that have hardened over centuries and begun to masquerade as fact, as truth. This has created structures of authority, resulted in conflicts and power play and turned religion and politics into fascist forces that legitimise violence.

We need to pause here and ask ourselves if all the faiths and ideologies we have created have enabled us to live intelligently and in peace. Could it be that we have been searching for something that doesn't exist? Could it be something like the horizon which appears reachable sooner or later, but as we move forward, seems to shift farther away from us?

The fact is that the horizon doesn't exist. It is an optical illusion. Our search for the meaning of life is futile. Yet we seem unable to stop ourselves from looking for it. Since the horizon is a mirage, the question of reaching it sooner or later doesn't arise. This constant struggle to live up to our ideas and beliefs, as I said earlier, is draining our energy. We are perhaps not honest enough to accept that humans exist for no nobler purpose compared with other animals such as ants and monkeys. But is it really so difficult to accept that and live in harmony with the world?

Many people believe that everyone must have their basic needs (food, shelter and health) met, and that they should also have the opportunity to pursue their interests or freely express themselves. But these are not goals as much as essential existential needs.

Perhaps there is no higher purpose to our existence than living fully and truthfully. To live truthfully is important because it will save us from falling for ideas that divide life into irreconcilable binaries of material and spiritual, good and evil.

This can only restrict our lives within narrow confines. All ideas, whether they come from religious or political discourses or texts, are subjective, and cannot capture the beauty and mystery of life within their frameworks. A life lived truthfully and to one's potential is its own reward. Perhaps that is the only meaning and purpose to our existence on this planet.

Despite our tremendous material progress and intellectual growth over centuries, our situation is not very different from that of the Kalamas of Kosala, who faced similar existential problems. They sought a way out of their dilemma from the Buddha, who happened to be passing through their city. The Buddha told them:

> Listen, Kalamas. Do not believe something just because it has been passed along and retold for many generations, because it has become a traditional practice, because it is well-known everywhere, or it is common opinion, because it is what the scriptures say, because it sounds logical, because it accords with your philosophy, because the speaker seems trustworthy.
>
> When you know for yourselves that these things are akusala, unskilful, these things when performed and undertaken conduce to ruin and sorrow, then reject them.
>
> And, Kalamas, when you know for yourselves that these things are kusala, skilful, when performed and undertaken, conduce to well-being and happiness, then live and act accordingly.

It is true that our lives are probably more complicated than it would have been during the Buddha's time. But then the human condition hasn't changed much and human emotions remain the same. Just that anger, envy, spite, greed and propensity to violence have only increased and manifest in more complex ways now.

The Buddha's principles are simple to follow. They call upon people to use their intelligence to distinguish between thoughts and actions that foster well-being and those that cause conflict and suffering.

All actions that have their roots in greed, hatred and delusion spring from self-centredness, a search for permanence and the harmful delusion of the self. They are akusala kamma, unskilful actions that produce sorrow. On the other hand, all efforts undertaken with generosity, love and wisdom, are kusala kamma, which are conducive to health and happiness.

Our task is to honestly figure out what constitutes skilful and unskilful actions in our everyday interactions with people and the world. That is how we will learn to cultivate friendliness, kindness and truthfulness. They will free us from hatred, spite and fear, and move us towards a state of happiness and freedom. We do so not because it is a commandment from a god, or something forbidden by the scriptures, but because unskilful actions drain our energy and make us unhappy.

II
God

WE WATCH THE DARK CLOUDS IN THE SKY AND THE rain that follows, cooling the ground. We see plants producing new leaves, trees blooming with flowers, a child burbling with laughter and we wonder how all this happened. Who created this beautiful life on earth? Surely it must be some all-powerful, all-knowing god. But who created god? And what really is god?

Of course, the idea of god cannot be discussed in a singular term, for there have always been numerous such ideas through history. As Karen Armstrong, a historian of religion, has said:

> The statement: 'I believe in God' has no objective meaning, as such, but like any other statement it only means something in context, when proclaimed by a particular community. Consequently, there is not one unchanging idea contained in the word 'God' but the word contains a whole spectrum of meanings, some of which are contradictory or even mutually exclusive. When one conception of God has ceased to have

> meaning or relevance, it has been quietly discarded and replaced by a new theology. A fundamentalist would deny this, since fundamentalism is anti-historical: it believes that Abraham, Moses and the later prophets all experienced their God in exactly the same way as people do today. Yet if we look at our three religions (Judaism, Christianity, and Islam), it becomes clear that there is no objective view of 'God': each generation has to create the image of God that works for them.

Indeed, ancient paintings, carvings, myths and legends should tell us that those who came before us worshipped not just one god but several. There was particular interest in worshipping the sky god and a mother goddess in certain ancient cultures. However, as Joseph Campbell and Karen Armstrong have shown in their works, there is a radical difference in the historic emergence and development of the idea of god(s) in the East and the West. It is a fascinating story which is too complex and layered to talk about here. Suffice to say that god in the West is primarily viewed as 'transcendental' and in the East as 'immanent'.

Proof of the Existence of God

Over the centuries, theologians and philosophers have provided several arguments to prove the existence of god. But in this book, we shall consider the three most famous arguments: ontological, cosmological and teleological.

- Ontological argument is analytic, yet it is an a priori judgement, that is, a position involving deductive reasoning. It means that since we do conceive of a god, a powerful entity, it implies that such a being exists.

- Cosmological argument is the causal argument. It proposes that there is something from which flora, fauna, human beings and the world evolved. All these cannot arise from nothing. And that is god. God is the ultimate explanation and the cause of everything. According to the cosmological argument, the necessary being—god—must exist and everything is contingent on that.
- Teleological argument is essentially an argument by design and order. If there is a watch, there must be a watchmaker and there must be a purpose behind making it. That is one of the more famous teleological arguments. Similarly, when we study nature—its order, beauty, unity and design—we believe that there is a great supernatural power and purpose behind its creation.

There are many powerful arguments against the existence of god as well. Here are a few:

- The theory that the so-called proofs verify nothing. They don't offer sufficient reason to believe in a supernatural being.
- If there was incontrovertible evidence of the existence of god, what need would we have for faith?
- If there is indeed a creator, then it is a terrible one. There is endless suffering in the world along with natural disasters like earthquakes and cyclones. Creation is not only a song of beauty, elegance and order but also a dirge of tragedies and horrors.

- If there is a cause for everything, then what caused the existence of god? If the belief is that god has been existing forever, then why not consider the universe as uncaused and eternal?

Atheism

The arguments for the existence of god or a supernatural power do not establish anything concrete because the evidence we have so far is not sufficient. Further, the religious experiences that people claim to have are personal and subjective. That speaks a lot about the nature of human experiences and not the nature of reality or god.

Atheism is not a refusal of the mystery of the universe; it is a rejection of the monopoly that religion holds over it. Atheism is also a refusal to accept faith without adequate evidence and so, a refusal to submit to a god who does not exist.

Agnosticism

People who identify as agnostic view attempts to answer metaphysical questions about god as a waste of precious time and energy. Human thought, given its nature and limited ability, cannot understand the ultimate reality, even if it exists. So why affirm or deny something that cannot be known or proved? Therefore, it's best to just let things go and get on with living.

Different Gods: Judaism, Christianity, Islam

The god of Abrahamic religions, namely, Judaism, Christianity and Islam, is a transcendental male god. He is eternal, the first cause, the prime mover, omnipotent and omniscient. And this supreme merciful god intervenes in the affairs of the humans, the acme of his creation, directly or by inspiration, through both scriptures and his messengers.

Since god is distinct from the universe, man's salvation can come only through surrender to god and obedience to his covenant. The goal of human life, therefore, is not to see or experience god in the here and now, but to surrender to his will.

While this belief is in all three religions, new discourses on god have taken place too. Over the centuries, mystics, saints and poets have played an instrumental role in this transformation of the conception and experience of god.

History is sprinkled with numerous Jewish, Christian and Islamic mystics and poets who have experienced and passed along a taste of the infinite vastness of life through their teachings and poems. More importantly, they brought God Yahweh, Heavenly Father and Allah, respectively, closer to their followers by making god a friend, lover and companion. Some mystics, who may be called non-dualists, went further and yearned for an immediate and direct experience of the divine. A few of them were put to death by the conservative forces within Christianity and Islam. However, these mystics remain a model for the highest state of being a person can reach.

Rapt in contemplation of the great unity of being, almost in the style of an Upanishadic seer declaring, 'Aham Brahmasmi' (I am Brahman), Mansur Al-Hallaj, the Persian mystic, asserted, 'Ana al-ḥaqq' (I am the Truth). It is also translated as 'I am God.' Rumi, Hafiz Shiraz, Saadi, Omar Khayyam and Ibn al-Arabi were other famous non-dual Sufi mystics and poets who offered believers a taste of the unity of being and were instrumental in making Islam popular around the world.

In Christianity, Meister Eckhart stands out as a mystic-poet. His mystical utterance, 'The Eye with which I see God is the same Eye with which God sees me,' suggests the non-dual experience has dazzled many Advaita Vedantins. Eckhart remains one of the most favourite mystics among the proponents of new-age spirituality.

Hinduism

The followers of Hinduism, which is also referred to as Sanātana Dharma, believe in not just one but hundreds of gods. While the idea that Hindus believe in thirty-three million gods is an exaggeration, that elaborate claim only means that there is tremendous freedom in Hinduism for each one to believe in or invent their own deity and worship them.

In reality, however, they worship predominantly two gods, Vishnu and Shiva, and their many manifestations under different forms and names. Add to this list the belief in Lakshmi, the goddess of wealth; Saraswati, the goddess of learning; and Durga, Parvati and Kali in their ugra (ferocious and aggressive) forms, symbolising destruction, fear and violence, and in their saumya (gentle and endearing) forms, depicting joy, knowledge and harmony.

Deities such as Yellamma, Maramma and many others under various other forms and names, are worshipped as grama devata (village deities). They may or may not be seen as manifestations of Durga or Parvati. Paravati's son, Ganesha or Vinayaka, the hugely popular elephant god, who is widely revered as the remover of obstacles and a bringer of good luck.

A *murti* of a god, statue, generally made by carving stone or wood, is believed to carry spiritual value. To many, a murti installed in a temple may even be an embodiment of the divine. Yet behind it all is the belief that god is one and it is formless and nameless. Among the murtis, Shivalinga is the most peculiar, revered variously as a phallic symbol, a pillar of light or as the form of the formless Shiva.

Finally, there is the notion of Brahman, not to be confused with Brahma, the Creator God. It is derived from the Sanskrit root 'brh' which means 'to grow, to swell, to enlarge', suggesting something that expands ceaselessly and is eternal.

Brahman is the supreme existence or absolute reality. It is invoked with the utterance of the word 'Om', or the primordial word 'vak'. It is sat (existence), chit (awareness), ananda (bliss)—the source of all matter, energy, time, space, being and everything of and beyond this visible universe. It is also personified as the One, or as the Person, saguna Brahman (Brahman as a god with attributes).

Brahman is beyond words; it is indescribable. Since it is not in the realm of knowledge, it is described as neti, neti, 'not this, not this', or as a negative space. Yet, paradoxical as it may sound, Brahman is realisable. We desire to know Brahman because of its presence within us. The human is constitutively immortal, that is, they are already Brahman. And to realise that is the goal of all spirituality. Moksha, *jivanmukti* and *sahaja sthithi* are some other terms used to refer to the state of Brahman.

Buddhism

The Buddha was not an atheist. While some Buddhist traditions may talk about deities and supernatural entities, there is no idea of a monotheistic god as found in other religions. The Buddha did not affirm or reject the existence of god, for there was simply no need for god. It is pointless to discuss whether god or a higher being of self exists because even if it exists, it cannot be known. It is *avyakta*, inexpressible. For, in the non-dual state of being where the binary or divided mind is absent, who can tell what it is and what it is not? Therefore, all assertions or affirmations about god, the Buddha said, are projections of a mind that is still being formed, and thus subject to suffering and rebirth. However, it is possible to end suffering. Once the separation of self from others and the world has ended, which is the cause of suffering, then we will understand everything.

Science and God

Scientists believe it is not in the domain of science to either prove or disprove the existence of a higher power, nor does it have the tools for it. Science can only study and attempt to explain the natural world. I do not mean to say that scientists do not believe in god—a lot of them do. It is said that a large section of scientists believe in some form of higher power.

The Higgs boson particle, named after scientist Peter Higgs, is also called 'the God particle'. It is supposed to have given mass to all matter after the Big Bang. The 'God particle' nickname has been criticised by many scientists because they do not think it explains the origin of the universe or its cause. Nonetheless, the chase for the elusive fundamental particle and the theory of everything persists.

A new idea called 'consciousness' entered the world of science, especially after the discovery of quantum mechanics in the 1920s, which revealed that the observer somehow influences the behaviour of particles. For much of the late nineteenth and twentieth centuries, scientists believed that it was not within their purview to inquire into the nature and function of consciousness; that it was not a fitting topic for 'serious science'. However, the discovery of interconnected quantum particles, also known as quantum entanglement in the early twentieth century, changed it all and there is now a broad agreement that the problem of consciousness is a serious scientific issue. The 'observer', who was on the margins of scientific method and discourse, moved to the centre of the scientific world.

A couple of major things took place: the question of how a grey, jelly-like lump of tissue in the head (the brain) with a hundred billion neurons give rise to consciousness, became one of the great scientific challenges of our time. And secondly, a significant number of scientists began believing that it is likely that consciousness is inherent in even the tiniest piece of particle, and it (bordering on the idea of god as an all-pervasive Brahman) is the source of all matter, energy, time, space and being.

This theory is generally referred to as panpsychism. According to it, consciousness is not some purely biological process generated in the brain. It is fundamental and ubiquitous. Consciousness, hence, is not limited to human beings but is a pervasive feature of the entire universe.

The Problem of Evil

The notion of evil is inextricably connected to faith in god and to the belief in saviours or prophets as embodiment of the good. Hence, the battle between the forces and the presumed triumph of good over evil. But if there is no evil, there is no good. In that case, the good god becomes irrelevant and saviours non-existent.

Going by the scholarly works of Joseph Campbell and others, it is quite likely that the idea of evil, in fact, of life itself as a conflict between the forces of darkness and light was a Zoroastrian belief that was later adopted by Judaism and Christianity. The Persian Zoroaster was probably the earliest prophet to have proposed that the world is a compound of Ahura Mazda (righteous order, light) and Angra Mainyu (evil principle), and that they are in a continuous battle. 'This concept of the battle between light and darkness,' Campbell writes, 'and the coming of a messiah to restore the pristine order, was in Achaemenian empire of Cyrus the Great (529 BC) and Darius I (521–486 BC), which later spread to India and Greece. The second manifestation of it was to be seen in the Hebrew religion, then in Christianity, and lastly in Islam.'

How this mythic order was borrowed and configured in different religions of the East and West would certainly make an enlightening story. But that is not within the scope of this book. However, it should serve our purpose here to point out that two types of evils were identified:

a. Moral evil emanating from cruel acts of human beings, whether wilful or otherwise, such as inflicting injury, killing, rape and destruction. All of these can be triggered by envy, anger, hatred and revenge; and
b. Natural evil or destruction caused by earthquakes, famines, hurricanes and other such disasters. Life, therefore, is a mix of tragedies and joy.

The presence of evil is inconsistent with the notion of god, who is supposed to be all-knowing and merciful. Therefore, a question that is often asked: How can a god, who is the embodiment of love and perfection, create a world where there is no freedom from pain, distress, suffering and violence?

The Traditional Christian Arguments

a. Evil is caused by Satan to undo and destroy god's plan and his covenant with humans.
b. The presence of evil is not god's fault, neither is it because of some imperfection in creation. God gave humans free will. Crime, war, terror, rape and other such harsh realities are all acts of human beings, who abuse free will. Having given free will to humans, god cannot interfere in any suffering caused by people's wrong choices.
c. Both natural evil and moral evil are the consequences of the sin Adam and Eve committed. Their wilful act of eating the forbidden fruit of knowledge led to the fall of man and corrupted the perfect world created by god.
d. Suffering has a redemptive value in our broken world. It helps us realise our weaknesses and accept the sins we have committed. We will continue to suffer because perfection exists only in the kingdom of god, which will be ours if we surrender to him and seek his mercy for salvation.

Response to the Problem of Evil in Hinduism

Hinduism is a complex religion with several traditions and schools of thought. So the problem of evil is different from how followers of Judaism, Christianity and Islam see it. Here are some major views that Hinduism has about evil:

a. An independent evil force such as Satan does not exist; there is only good and bad karma. Wrong actions stem from *ahamkara*, an egoic mind, or the self which creates the illusion of separateness and permanence. Interestingly, the epics tell us the stories about the marvellous play of ego in both the celestial and human worlds. This becomes the reason for manifestation of life, and sets the ball of samsara (the cycle of birth, death and eventual liberation) rolling.
b. A story goes that once upon a time, the gods and the demons came together for *samudra manthana*, that is, to churn the heavenly ocean to recover *amrita*, the elixir of immortality. During the churning, several things sprang out, the first of which was halahala, a deadly poison that seemed to threaten to destroy the world. Shiva drank it and froze it in his throat, paving the way for the wonderful gifts of life to emerge thereafter. The churning of the ocean symbolises the birth and cycle of samsara, which bring in its wake anxiety, anger, pride, despair and a deep yearning to know the secret of existence. What followed was a lesson on the importance of neutralising passions that pull life down and then reaching a state of immortality—a cessation of delusions, fear and separation.
c. What causes suffering is karma, thoughts and actions played out from one's past or present life. Karma produces both joy and sorrow. We cannot escape its consequences unless we tread the path of righteousness that is grounded in the ability to distinguish right from wrong.

d. Suffering is an innate part of living, of samsara.
e. There is no evil, no suffering, no death and no liberation; it is all maya, an illusion, caused by ignorance.

The Buddhist Perspective on Evil

Buddha's story of awakening is presented as an event of intense struggle and conflict, as a battle against Mara, whose army consisted of his three sons, Flurry, Gaiety and Pride, and three daughters, Discontent, Delight and Thirst. Mara's army tried to dislodge the Buddha's solemn purpose with temptation. Eventually, however, the army was defeated and Mara fled the Buddha's mind. Some European scholars have interpreted the Buddha's struggle as a battle between good and evil. That is not correct. The Buddha overcame what is called *klesha*, afflictions of the egoic mind, such as ignorance, desire and attachment to samsara, and fear of the unknown. These kleshas do not have maleficent powers nor are they independent forces. They are barriers one needs to overcome to lead a good life and eventually attain freedom.

III
Religion

THERE IS NO CONSENSUS ON WHAT EXACTLY constitutes a religion, for there are so many different ones around the world. While some like Islam have faith in one god, others worship multiple gods. And then there are religions like Animism that have no notion of god at all, instead, there is the belief that the entire universe is pervaded by a spirit which is in everything—animals, plants, mountains, rivers, humans—energising them and giving them direction.

Most religions have their own worldviews, sacred narratives and scriptures, symbols and rituals, prophets or messengers, festivals, funeral rituals, music, art, ethics and, most prominently, a belief in a personal god or gods. Some of the major religions of the world are Buddhism, Jainism, Hinduism, Judaism, Confucianism, Christianity, Islam, Shintoism, Sikhism, Taoism, Zoroastrianism and Bahaism. Some indigenous American religions and African religions are practised as well. Orthodox believers often claim that fundamental beliefs in god, the scriptures, sacred symbols and places have remained the same over centuries, but all religions have evolved over time. These changes have been brought about by religious leaders in light of their experiences, by self-seeking clerics as well as critical insiders and mystics.

We do not know how and when religion originated. To hazard a theory, perhaps it started when the early human evolved into a thinking–feeling subject, began to feel disconnected from the totality of life and wondered about their place in the universe. This is just my guess. But what we do know for sure is that religion functions simultaneously on several levels:

- as a set of beliefs about the cosmic order, world and life;
- as a set of symbols, rites and sacraments;
- as fear and devotion to something that is considered supernatural, god, beyond our control and comprehension; and
- as a deep impulse to transcend our ordinary, divided self that is entrenched in deep conflict, fear and a sense of lack.

The Philosophy and Politics of Religions, Messengers of God and Related Issues

We may appreciate that god is truly a great diplomat for having sent out numerous messengers to inspire the formation of hundreds of religions, sacred narratives and scriptures. Unfortunately, that is not what some leaders and preachers of monotheistic religions think. Rather they claim that their religion alone is the true word of god, that only their scriptures are divine revelations and that all other gods, except their own, are false.

With such overassertive beliefs, monotheistic faiths have perpetrated great conflict and acts of violence that cannot be reduced to political and economic factors. Not just monotheistic faiths, any faith for that matter, whether it is Hinduism or Sikhism or even Buddhism, that claim monopoly over god, truth, mystery, would be intolerant towards other gods and faiths and other ways of being in the world.

Religions in general, and monotheistic faiths in particular, have also spawned a cruel gender hierarchy. Those who believe in gender equality quite rightly find that the idea of one truth, one god along with the image of god as male have seeded and strengthened patriarchal values and continue to be a source of oppression of and violence towards women. In the words of Mary Daly, radical feminist philosopher: 'The image of God as exclusively a father and not a mother, for example, was spawned by the human imagination under the condition of patriarchal society and sustained as plausible by patriarchy. Then, in turn, the image has served to perpetuate this kind of society by making its mechanisms for the oppression of women appear right and fitting.'

In some religions, such as Hinduism for example, goddesses are worshipped as powers of the universe, as creative energies and, simultaneously, as destructive and liberating forces. In reality, however, the position of women in Hindu society is lower than men's. The domesticated woman, be it a mother, a wife or a daughter, may, however, be put on a pedestal and applauded. While female worshippers like Akka Mahadevi, Lalleshwari and Meera Bai, who rejected patriarchal values and gender and caste hierarchies, are treated as saints, women who live normal, everyday lives continue to suffer discrimination and violence in every area of life.

It is true that religions have not remained static, not because they have undergone radical course correction from within, but because of the women's struggle for equality, dignity and autonomy and because of the marginalised people's rebellion against the oppressive values of the religious traditions.

The human mind understands the world in binaries. Religious thinking also follows this pattern. That is why some (if not all) religious discourses have two competing forces in its texts. For instance, matter and spirit, materiality and spirituality, body and soul, life and death and so on.

However, life does not function that way. It cannot be arranged in such neat categories. It is a unitary movement, in continuous flux. Cause and effect, life and death are simultaneous processes. Galaxies decay and perish, and new ones are formed. Plants and animals die and are replaced by new shoots and offspring, respectively. Similarly, human beings pass away and usher in a new generation of people. This process is nature's way of balancing and sustaining the universe's ecosystem. One cannot exist without the other: it is all a simultaneous, unitary process. But we divide up life into different sections, into material and spiritual, life and death as disconnected events, and get trapped within our concepts. Soon, we start to believe in them as unyielding, hard realities of life.

So, can a religion that was formed at a time when knowledge and experience of life was limited, when the language in which it was expressed was entrenched in binaries, be capable of change? Can it shed its divisive beliefs and practices and knock down all borders created by denominational identity and politics? Can such a religion be the voice of freedom? Can it reinvent itself in light of the teachings of the sages, mystics and poet-saints, who have given us a taste of the infinite vastness of life that can never be captured in texts and discourses? Can spirituality, the way of these sages and mystics, be a way out of religious conflict and bigotry?

Since prehistoric times, humans have believed that there are extraordinary people among them who can communicate with spirits, connect with god, bring messages from the other world, heal the sick and predict the future. Take the example of shamanism among hunter–gatherer cultures that farming societies continued to follow. It is associated with indigenous and tribal societies to this day.

A shaman is regarded as one who has access to the world of both good and evil spirits. Usually, the shaman enters a state of trance before they begin to exhibit their powers. They are said to answer questions about the living and dead, warn of upcoming dangers, heal the sick and even escort the souls of the dead to the other world. Believing in shamans' capabilities allayed people's fears and gave them a sense of refuge. As time progressed, what were once cults developed into full-blown religions. They began to receive royal patronage and shamans became prophets, messiahs and saviours.

Shamanism strengthened the belief that the world is more than what it appears to be. That there are unseen, incomprehensible forces influencing our life. That there are people gifted with abilities and can travel between the worlds to bring back messages of great significance. This belief has spawned the imagination of all religions and shaped their discourse.

The terms 'messenger', 'messiah' and 'prophet' are wrongly used as synonyms. Messiah means the anointed one who is a saviour. A messenger is a spiritual being through whom god communicates with believers. A prophet is a special messenger, who brings to the human world divine revelations that eventually become the basis for scriptures. Depending on the religion, messengers and prophets hold more important positions when compared with the other. Perhaps because there were so many messiahs and prophets that, at some stage, it became crucial for self-appointed persons or groups, with the backing of political power, to proclaim that their prophet was the only one who mattered.

It signifies an attempt to monopolise 'divine utterances' under one name and in one book. It is also a desperate measure to consolidate the group's hold on its followers. Perhaps their intention was genuine, in that they believed they were really doing god's work. However, it also was a mark of arrogance to insist that they had some special insights into the secret of existence and that only theirs was the one real messenger of god, especially in a world where various philosophies, cultures, languages and gods thrive.

In Hinduism, 'avatar' means a manifestation of the divine. There are two types of avatars. The first is an incarnation of one aspect of god and is called a partial avatar. Second, *poorna* avatar is the complete incarnation of god itself in the flesh. The purpose of the avatar is to instruct people about the right path, destroy wicked forces that cause disorder, restore balance in the world and establish dharma on firm grounds.

Christianity has its version of avatar as well. There is a belief that god became flesh in the form of Jesus to destroy the power of the devil, enable people to partake in the divine nature and realise the depth of god's love. However, both Judaism and Islam reject the doctrine of god's incarnation in flesh or any form.

Since there is no belief in god in Buddhism, the thought of an incarnation of god does not arise at all. There is, of course, the idea of Bodhisattva. Bodhisattva, or Maitreya Buddha, is one who attains supreme enlightenment, not merely for personal sake but for all sentient beings, and returns to the world to lead humanity to freedom and happiness. According to another theory, a Bodhisattva is an enlightened being who, out of compassion, forgoes or postpones their own final nirvana to help others reach the state of enlightenment.

Talking about messiahs and avatars, Joseph Campbell says: 'The tribal or local heroes perform their deeds for a single folk, and universal heroes like Mohammed, Jesus, and Buddha bring the message from afar. These heroes of religion came back with the wonder of God, not with a blueprint of God.'

This is a creative way of understanding these extraordinary persons, as ones who searched for the truth. And when they came upon it, their perception of life was radically altered.

They then returned to the world to share their insights with the common folk. In other words, they were indeed the 'messengers of god' or 'saviours'—not in the orthodox religious and exclusive sense of the term, fixed in time and space; rather, in the sense that they bring home the wonder and mystery of life, indicating the *possibility* of ending sorrow, and of transcending the binary or divided self, which is the cause of all conflict and sorrow.

Aurobindo, a mystic-philosopher, had a unique way of looking at such incarnations of god. According to him, the lives and teaching of avatars certainly worked as turning points in history, that is, as catalysts for the emergence or development of a new consciousness. But then, even such an advancement in life, over a period of time, may degenerate into rigid or dogmatic ways of being and doing things in the world and thus create the need for yet another intervention, the arrival of yet another avatar.

Are Scriptures the Words of God?

Scriptures are believed to be written accounts of the teachings that god had shared via a prophet, painstakingly put together by their disciples over generations.

The Old and New Testaments in the form of accounts, hymns, parables, sermons and prophecies were derived orally and then pieced together by different apostles. The Old Testament is believed to have been completed around 100 CE. The Bible's first gospel was written down some forty years after the death of Jesus Christ, but the New Testament, with all the four gospels, was composed almost a hundred years after his passing. Writing down the Quran was also a long and laborious task. Verses that had been uttered by Prophet Mohammad over the course of twenty-three years were compiled more than hundred years after his death.

The prophets were not the authors of these sacred texts, and the disciples who collated their words were not seers or sages but ordinary human beings, subject to weakness and error. They compiled the teachings without offering any comment even if what was being said was contradictory. They may even have unwittingly inserted their fears, hopes and aspirations into the texts. We also cannot discount that these holy texts were written at a time of limited knowledge about the world.

All of these elements make the scriptures not divine and infallible, but human. That partly explains the inconsistencies, ambiguities and contradictions in them, giving room for multiple interpretations of the text, resulting in diverse beliefs. And, not surprisingly, this difference in the texts has been effectively used by several groups to claim their version of the faith as authentic, and then go on to defend and proselytise their point of view, even silencing those who do not agree with them.

In Buddhism, the Pali Canon, also known as the Tripitaka—three baskets—is not considered the word of god or a revelation, but as a repository of the Buddha's teachings. The Buddhavachana, words of or discourses by the Buddha, include his life story. The thing to note here is that the Buddha is not regarded as an avatar or a messiah or a prophet. He is, instead, a divine being worthy of worship and emulation because he (re)discovered dhamma as the way to end sorrow.

In Hinduism, the Vedas are considered *apauruseya*, authorless or not human. But the ideas of the Vedas as the only source of valid knowledge was a Brahmanical invention. Since almost all Brahmins knew Sanskrit and, as such, had access to these texts, they sought spiritual authority for themselves. The Vedas certainly are inspired texts, but they were composed by several minds and passed on from generation to generation before they were written down. The Vedas, Upanishads, the Bhagavad Gita and the Brahmasutras do have scriptural value, but the practice and significance of Hinduism is not entirely dependent on them. There are several spiritual traditions that do not refer to these texts at all. In fact, sages, mystics and saint-poets are considered greater spiritual authorities by many.

Scriptures and Sacred Books as Unfinished Texts

Messengers, messiahs and avatars marked a turning point in the history of religion. These extraordinary human beings helped to radically change the way people viewed and experienced the world. But they did not offer a blueprint that could be followed by future generations.

The evolution of human beings is an ongoing story. Hence, religious texts that humans have constructed through imagination, fear, hope, inspiration and aspiration are unfinished too. They are, at best, profound beginnings, and not the final answers to all our questions. Nor are they the solutions to our problems. Accepting this fact makes us humble, keeps us open-minded, ready to learn and make necessary changes as we move along in life.

What Is Spirituality?

In our heart of hearts, we know that life and the world around us are not what they appear to be, that there is something greater than ourselves. Spirituality is a quest to know and experience that great mystery. It is not a dismissal of the importance of religions or its sacred texts; rather it is a deep hunger to know directly, without the mediation of a text or any authority, everything about the great unknown.

The popular understanding of spirituality, which has been invented and perpetrated by gurus or godmen, or clerics in religious institutions, is in direct contradiction to the actual or living spirit of spirituality. Unfortunately, the term 'spiritual' is often used to describe anything associated with the spirit, in contrast to the body or to material and physical matters. Almost all our religious and spiritual discourses are stuck in this dichotomy between spirit and matter, body and soul, spirituality and materiality. And that has split our lives into two ever-conflicting parts.

It is all one; we cannot divide life into material and spiritual. It is the dualistic nature of the self that divides life into material and spiritual, good and evil, body and mind, beauty and ugly, sacred and profane. Taking up a job or starting a business to earn a living does not make a person materialistic, any more than going to a temple, meditating or studying a religious text makes them spiritual. The self that is involved in both the so-called material and spiritual activities is the same: seeking security, pleasure, meaning, purpose and an anchor in one's life. In other words, materialism and spiritualism are two sides of the same coin that people seek to overcome a sense of lack or incompleteness.

So, without privileging spiritual hunger over physical desires, it is critical to understand that these words, 'spiritual' and 'materialistic', are functional terms with functional meanings. They only explain the interests and activities of a person.

Nowadays, spirituality is often associated with yoga, meditation and the well-being of body, mind and spirit, while religion is related to an institutionalised belief system with an explicit denominational identity. But what is becoming more and more popular is new-age spiritualty that is characterised as being anti-institutional, personal, inclusive and universal.

Spirituality without Religion and God

At a deeper level, this new-age spirituality is both a critique of organised religions—their narrow, chauvinistic belief systems and their judgemental god—and an attempt to develop an inclusive and universal movement without the need for religious identity, structure or monotheism. Its adherents may retain a belief in god or a higher power, and derive their inspiration from thinkers of all religions and cultures, including modern science. It is a new theology of liberation, so to speak, without borders and religious dogma, and the discarding of linear, reductionist theories of life and body-mind-spirit. This spirituality is a deep faith in the inextricable interconnectedness of all things and the possibility of every individual realising their potential.

It is also sometimes referred to as 'secular' spirituality, because its philosophy is about oneness with nature and connecting one's inner self with the outer world. In a way, this spirituality is a way of being and doing things that spark love and joy.

The story of Jesus Christ in D.H. Lawrence's last work of fiction in 1930, *The Man Who Died*, can serve as a pointer to this new kind of spirituality. The story is an unconventional reworking of the traditional story of Jesus Christ's resurrection. A powerful and moving tale, it compels us to interrogate the grand narratives we have been fed since childhood.

Let us recapitulate the story in brief: One evening, inside the cave where the body of Jesus was kept, he wakes up and, despite the pain he feels all over, manages to wrap a linen sheet around himself. He then walks out of the cave and away from the town. In Lawrence's evocative prose: 'He slowly followed the road away from the town, past the olives, under which purple anemones were drooping in the chill of dawn . . . he went on, on scarred feet, neither of this world nor of the next. Neither here nor there, neither seeing nor yet sightless, he passed dimly on, away from the city and its precincts, wondering why he should be travelling, yet driven by a dim, deep nausea of disillusion, and a resolution of which he was not even aware.'

He then takes shelter in a peasant's house: '"Don't be afraid," he assures the frightened man, "I am not dead. They took me down too soon. So I have risen up. Yet if they discover me, they will do it all over again."

The next day, he meets with Madeleine, who, recovering from her initial shock, asks, "Will you come back?"

Jesus replies, "What is finished is finished, and for me the end is past . . . the teacher and the saviour are dead in me; now I can go about my business, into my own single life."

"Have you risen for yourself alone?"

"I have not risen from the dead in order to seek death again," Jesus answers tartly.

And he walks away from the place, thinking thus: "What a pity I preached to them! A sermon is so much more likely to cake into mud, and to close the fountains, than is a psalm or a song. I made a mistake. I understand that they executed me for preaching to them. Yet they could not finally execute me, for now I am risen in my own aloneness, and inherit the earth, since I lay no claim on it."

Towards the end of the first part of the story, healed of his wounds, Jesus asks himself a last question: 'From what, and to what, could this infinite whirl be saved?'

In the second part of the book, he meets Isis and they live like man and woman for a brief period. And once 'the man and the woman were fulfilled of one another,' he leaves Isis, telling her: 'If I stay, they will betray me to the Romans and to their justice. But I will never be betrayed again. So when I am gone, live in peace with the growing child. And I shall come again: all is good between us, near or apart. The suns come back in their seasons: and I shall come again.'

Jesus moves away from the old path not for a better life, but for a new life without a necessary end. He is not a messiah or a prophet who has risen to complete his mission, but a carpenter's son aspiring to live his life fully. There are no grand goals to achieve—whether religious or political—except to be alive and to live wholly because all goals are false.

And so Lawrence's Jesus refuses to have anything to do with religion and walks away from his messiahship, to seek fulfilment in the ordinariness of life. Shedding his missionary goal, he becomes himself, to be alive in the flesh, 'to be most vividly, most perfectly alive' like the 'flower and beast and bird'. To be part of the sun, the earth, the sea, the living incarnate cosmos.

IV
Body, Mind and Soul

WE GENERALLY PRESUME THAT WE KNOW ALL about the body, mind and soul or spirit; especially about the body–mind unit that appears to be solid and real, like the trees, hills and houses. As regards the soul or spirit, it may remain invisible, intangible, yet we are certain that it exists, because all religions and gurus have talked about how the human being is not merely a body, a bundle of flesh and bones that is subject to decay and death, rather the human being is something more, something that is pristine, nobler, higher and divine.

A non-dualist mystic or poet might say the triumvirate—body, mind and soul—are mere impressions; something like the waves in a sea that rise and drop and disappear, or like the passing clouds that appear for a while during a season, descend on earth as water and then evaporate, and what is left is the empty, infinite, burning sky.

A postmodern deconstructionist may call our body–mind composite a metaphysical construct, that is, both the mind and the body are not something that's given, like the trees and mountains that appear solid and real, but a significant effect of language. And that it is through language and in relation to things that we construct ourselves as the body–mind, plus or minus the soul.

Body-Mind

The body is the physical aspect of all life forms. The body of a mosquito or a tiger is seen as whole, complete. A tiger is its body with all its inherent instincts and drives; that is, its body and instincts are not considered as something separate or independent of each other. In contrast, the human body is considered as only the material form of a person and it is impermanent and corporeal, as opposed to the mind and soul. And there are many who think our bodies imperfect.

In fact, the human body is extremely fascinating. It is the microcosm of the universe. When we begin to understand it, we get a sense of its physical, chemical and biological processes as well as the workings of the planet and other life forms. An extraordinarily intelligent and resilient structure, it has survived over millions of years and thrived under all kinds of perilous conditions. The human body with the millions of cells that make it, including the brain, has a mind of its own. The body and mind are not identical yet not separate, for they are intricately linked. We cannot speak of the body without the mind, though *this mind is not the same as the self or ego*.

The Mind (capitalised hereafter), in the sense of intelligence, is present everywhere. As mentioned earlier, this is known as panpsychism. It is there in the seed of a tree as much as in a mosquito. It is present in matter, in every particle of the universe and in every cell of the body. This Mind may be understood as consciousness that is intelligence with no frontiers. We do not know if it has a beginning or an end or if it is eternal. However, this Mind as intelligence has to be distinguished from the human mind as self or ego.

Human Mind As Self, Ego

Life always finds a way. The heart beats, the liver functions and the senses operate without the exercise of the human will. The will, which is a feature of the self, is a movement different from that of the body—yet it is not outside the body. How and when the self emerged, which we also refer to as the human mind, ego or 'I', is unknown. It is believed that *Homo sapiens* evolved from their early predecessors two or three million years ago and then went on to develop a capacity for language, setting in motion the expansion of the self-conscious, self-reflexive human being. So, it is possible that with the invention of language, the 'I' developed and, over the centuries, the idea of the self has fortified and established itself as an independent entity.

The Bible says that the emergence of the self or the human mind as ego, which marked the loss of innocence and alienation from the totality of life, was caused when Adam and Eve ate the forbidden fruit of knowledge.

In Hinduism, desire is considered as the trigger for the emergence of 'I' or the ego, which, in effect, is consciousness acting as an independent entity. This also marked the beginning of samsara, the cyclicality of human existence.

In Buddhism, too, the human mind or the self is understood as *tanha*—thirst, desire, longing—which is the cause of both happiness and suffering, the cycle of becoming, *bhavachakra*, within which exists the deep impulse to transcend the separation and suffering as well.

According to modern Western psychology influenced by Sigmund Freud, the ego is one of the components of a personality. The other two are id (the primitive and instinctual part of the mind that contains sexual and aggressive drives) and super-ego (moral conscience). In other words, ego is the conscious mind that negotiates between the demands of the id, superego and reality. Ego is both a mediator and a negotiator, and its development enables a child to grow into an adult and develop a distinct personality. The ego is a mixed bag of qualities shaped by both biology and culture. While qualities such as love and empathy can lead to the overall healthy growth of the mind, negative propensities such as jealousy, hatred, fear and anger can lead one to destruction and sorrow.

What a perplexing piece of work is the ego self, which is at once creative and destructive! It is the inventor of religions, culture, politics, great architecture, wonderful artifacts and enchanting music. It is behind the great stories of heroes, artists, poets, rogues and villains. The ego is also the great seeker of truth. It is the same self, made up of memory, that is reading this text and trying to make sense of it. The story of the self is an incredible one. To quote a famous dialogue from a Hindi movie, '*Picture abhi baaki hai, mere dost*.' The story isn't over yet, my friend.

Does a Human Have a Soul?

Animism is the ancient belief that all creations—human beings, animals, plants, rivers, mountains and stars—are animated and alive, possessing a distinct spiritual essence. Indigenous people around the world did not, and still don't, believe in a single or multiple gods but in spirit as an integral part of the physical world. While some of the Asian religions retained the animistic aspect of nature worship, it was completely marginalised in Abrahamic religions, and in its place was installed the grand belief in a single, transcendental god as well as the concept of soul.

Of course, there isn't just one concept of soul; all religions have their own version of this complex idea. The Hindu notion of *atman* or Self (capitalised, not the small 'self', which is identified as the egoic mind or 'I') is different from the Christian or Islamic notion of the soul. Nonetheless, the common defining characteristic of these different ideas of the soul is that it is perceived as a separate conscious entity, and that in its complex relationship with god, mind and body, the soul is invariably favoured over the body. The soul is considered pure and transcendental; the body is mortal, subject to decay and death. The body has to be rejected and transcended so that the soul can be realised.

Body and Soul

Notwithstanding the attempts made by mystics and philosophers to overcome the hard dualism of body–soul and soul–god, the problematic divide between the body and soul continues to be the bedrock on which all religions are built, remaining at the heart of all their discourses even today.

Just as hate is perceived to be the enemy of love, the body is seen as the enemy of the soul. Religions might differ in their interpretations of the soul, but they all pit it against the body. Even the concept of atman, however differently it may be interpreted from the other notions of the soul, is not free of this counterproductive dichotomy. In Buddhism, there is no notion of soul, so the comparison between body and soul does not arise. Despite that, in several Buddhist traditions too, the body is viewed as a receptacle of disgusting discharges and stench, an impediment to nirvana.

In almost all religious discourses and narratives, while the soul has always been viewed as pure, higher, perfect and immortal, the body is thought of as impure. In a nutshell:

a. The body is something to be ashamed of, to be rejected and transcended in order to attain moksha or nirvana.
b. The body goes through cycles of births and deaths, until it finds release and becomes one with the supreme being. Or, after death, according to the Christian and Islamic doctrines, the body–soul remains in limbo, until it is resurrected and borne away to the other world by the grace of god.
c. The body in general is an object of disgust, exuding impure secretions. The female body in particular, is an embodiment of sexual corruption and distraction, which impedes spiritual growth.

The Body as a Field of Energy and Site of Liberation

For centuries, the understanding of the body, its nature and functions, was woefully limited at the time when scriptures and spiritual texts were composed. Hence, the attitude against the body in opposition to the mind and spirit or soul were such that it was hard to conceive transcendental states of being as having a neuro-physical basis. The spiritual texts and narratives, therefore, projected the body as an enemy in the spiritual quest, as an obstacle to enlightenment. In effect, matter was viewed as a burden, and therefore, liberation meant release from materialisation, from body/matter.

Classical science has presented matter and energy as separate entities. This, too, has contributed to the strengthening of the binary narratives of good and evil, spirituality and materiality, soul and body. But today, we have moved beyond these rigid black-and-white ideas in all aspects of life. We no longer consider matter and energy as two distinct aspects; we see them as a continuum. Interestingly, texts on Kundalini yoga, Tantra yoga and other such spiritual disciplines that developed in the first millennium in India discuss mental states, including higher states of consciousness that are related to energy centres in the body. The lives and teachings of mystics and sages such as Gopi Krishna, the Mother (of Pondicherry), Ramana Maharshi and U.G. Krishnamurti have offered us a radically different understanding of the body, both as a field of energy and as a channel of liberating force, which, when actualised, catapults the human into a state of unitary consciousness.

The body is not a mortal object. With death, thinking stops, thoughts cease and it is the end of a person's story. But we do not know if the human mind survives death with its memories intact and is then reincarnated into a new body. Does the soul continue to exist after death, or does it merge with some form of higher life? These are answers we do not have. But we do know that there is no death for the body, there is only a change of form. When clinical death takes place, the body breaks itself into its constituent elements which rejoin the flow of life. A rotting corpse discharges soil-enriching chemicals which nourish other life forms. Even when the dead body is cremated, the ash, if scattered on the earth, leads to the birth of tiny plants. The body remains within the flow of life. Nothing is lost. And there is no end to life.

Giving expression to the immortality of life, a hymn in the Rigveda (10.16.3), recited during the funeral, goes like this: 'May your eye go to the sun, your life's breath to the wind. Go to the sky or to earth as is your nature; or to the waters, if that is your destiny. Take root in the plants with your limbs.'

As the Buddha maintained, 'Within this fathom-long sentient body itself is the world, the arising of the world, the cessation of the world, and the path leading to the cessation of the world.'

This means that from the time the world arises—samsara—till the cessation of the self and sorrow which leads to nirvana, everything is within the matrix and play of the body. We can also add that within the body is the cosmic dance of life; in fact, the cosmos itself is the body. The following lines from the Bhagavad Gita, 'The atman cannot be cut, cannot be burnt, cannot be wetted, and also cannot be dried up,' is often quoted to assert that the soul is eternal, immovable and ancient. However, paradoxical as it may seem, the portrayal of the universal form of Lord Krishna in the text subverts the discourse on the soul and serves as a brilliant metaphor for the immortal, all-pervading body.

In the Gita, Krishna speaks about the different forms of yoga, and on the nature of Brahman and Atman and then bestows on Arjuna a vision of his universal form. Arjuna beholds the whole cosmos reflected in the seamless body of Krishna. All forms of life exist there, and at the centre of it all is Lord Brahma resting on a lotus, surrounded by sages and heavenly serpents. The sun, the moon and the heavenly planets blaze along, and worlds radiate within worlds in a never-ending kaleidoscope. Torrents of rivers flow relentlessly into thunderous seas, and the flaming mouth of Krishna devours all the worlds and its creatures. It is the body, boundless, with no beginning, middle or end, that is recreating itself in an endless maya of destruction and creation. In effect, the Gita espouses that the body is infinite and immortal.

Almost in line with the quoted Vedic hymn, Paul Davies, a noted physicist, offers a 'scientific' view of the immortality of life, of body/matter in particular, in his popular book *The Origin of Life*. He writes, 'Since the Earth formed, its material has not remained inert. Carbon, hydrogen, nitrogen and oxygen are continually recycled through the atmosphere and crust by geological and biological processes. When an organism dies and decays, its atoms are released back into the environment. Some of them eventually become part of other organisms. Simple statistics reveal that your body contains about one atom of carbon from every milligram of dead material more than 1,000 years old. This simple fact has amazing implications. You are, for example, host to a billion or so atoms that once belonged to Jesus Christ, or Julius Caesar, or the Buddha, or the tree that the Buddha once sat beneath.' Let us not hesitate to add even atoms that once belonged to the pharaohs or Adolf Hitler and Joseph Stalin. Perhaps we could even add to the list creatures such as the woolly mammoth, dodo and dinosaurs. There is no end to life, it only takes on new forms and new expressions.

V
Knowledge

THE URGE TO KNOW, THE ABILITY TO THINK abstractly and create symbols and words for what one has experienced is an innate human characteristic. Animals, on the other hand, lead a straightforward life. When they are joyous, they jump, run and dance. When in heat, they have sex. When they are injured, they lick their wounds, rest and get healed. And if that's not possible, they isolate themselves and breathe their last. There is no evidence so far of animals wondering about the mysteries of life and where they will go after death.

Humans are different because of their knowledge. We churn out ideas about life and death, god and beyond, religions and belief systems, politics and wars, art, music and literature. The human being sings both out of joy and sorrow, kills both out of love and hate, also tries to break free from all limitations and ideations to taste the infinite vastness of life. The human is a fantastic two-legged creature, the likes of which probably cannot be found anywhere else, at least not on the planets that revolve around the sun, like devotees around a temple.

The lives of the men who came millions of years before us were directed by their five senses and the innate instinct of survival. At some point in their evolution, they got the ability to make sounds and invent words. Thus began the story of the human quest for knowledge. The hominid had turned into a thinking animal.

For thousands of years, it is said, the early humans lived as hunters and gatherers of food. When they began to migrate in groups, settle on fertile lands and take to agriculture, their lives underwent a radical shift and led to the expansion of language and culture. Thousands of years later, there was yet another change in human consciousness. Between 2800 BCE and 2300 BCE, the coming of Zoroaster in Iran; the seers of the Upanishads, Mahavira and the Buddha in India; the Hebrew prophets in Israel; Confucius and Lao Tzu in China; and Pythagoras, Heraclitus, Socrates, Plato and Aristotle in Greece marked a pivotal period in human history that led to the development of religions and philosophical systems that continue to challenge and inspire human thought to this day.

Around 2,400 years ago, when Socrates said, 'An unexamined life is not worth living,' he developed the Socratic method, a dialogic, critical inquiry into life. With that, he, along with his disciples Plato and Aristotle, laid the foundation for the development of Western philosophy. For several centuries, much of the inquiry centred around the nature of reality, characteristics of the mind and its relation to the body, free will, god and moral and political philosophy. In the seventeenth century, almost over 2,000 years after Aristotle, Western thought, which had predominantly revolved around metaphysical ideas and Christian theology, was led in different directions. Rene Descartes, who is considered the founder of modern philosophy, spoke about rationalism. He did not believe that all knowledge is derived from sensory experiences; rather he thought that there were perceptions driven by intellect that were distinctly independent of the senses. Hence his famous statement 'Cogito, ergo sum,' or 'I think, therefore I am'. He advocated doubt as a method of inquiry to eliminate falsehood and arrive at the truth.

During the seventeenth and eighteenth centuries, during the Enlightenment movement, philosophers such as David Hume, Immanuel Kant, John Locke, Montesquieu, Jean-Jacques Rousseau and Voltaire ushered in new ways of thinking about knowledge and society. Three major ideas that rode high and steered modernity during this movement were reason, individualism and scepticism.

A century later, the works of Karl Marx and Fredrich Engels introduced a whole new philosophy. They argued that thinking abstractly about the world and life and producing ideas, however profound and revolutionary, was not going to change the world. Only actual activity and practices could do that. As they said, 'The philosophers have only interpreted the world, in various ways; the point is to change it.' The work of these two masters that came to be called Marxism was adopted by people working in various fields, such as anthropology, political science, history, sociology, cultural studies, education, economics, literary criticism, theatre and critical psychology. It remains one of the most powerful philosophies in the world today.

In the twentieth century, there was further shake-up in the world of Western philosophy. Ludwig Wittgenstein, Edmund Husserl, Martin Heidegger and Jean-Paul Sartre were some of the movers and shakers of this new philosophy, namely, phenomenology or philosophy of experience, which implied the lived experience is the source of all meaning and value we attribute to life.

What I find fascinating is that the history of Western philosophy has been a history of continuous tension between and among rationalists, empiricists, idealists, pragmatists, universalists, humanists, socialists and existentialists. Debates between different schools of thoughts have been a common occurrence. I wonder how Socrates would have reacted to these varied attempts at a critical examination of life and quest for knowledge. Would he have frowned with exasperation or smiled with satisfaction?

There was one man who we know for sure wasn't impressed. Friedrich Nietzsche thought that the very desire to understand the human being was a way to control people. He criticised Western philosophy and the Christian faith in particular when he wrote: 'What then is truth? A mobile army of metaphors, metonyms, and anthropomorphisms—in short, a sum of human relations which have been enhanced, transposed, and embellished poetically and rhetorically, and which after long use seem firm, canonical, and obligatory to a people: truths are illusions about which one has forgotten that this is what they are; metaphors which are worn out and without sensuous power; coins which have lost their pictures and now matter only as metal, no longer as coins.' The scathing critique was followed by a declaration: 'God is dead', rendering a death blow to the very foundation of the Western philosophy. It exposed the deep rot that had set in orthodox Christianity and unleashed limitless play, meaning there can be no predetermined limitations or fixed answers.

Gilles Deleuze, Jacques Derrida, Michel Foucault, Richard Rorty, Jean-Francois Lyotard were some of the notable inheritors of Nietzsche's legacy and carried forward the demolition act and limitless play of his anti-philosophy. The death of god marked the end of epistemology-centred philosophy. Suddenly it was found, to the glee and consternation of many practising thinkers, that there were no objective facts, no immaculate perceptions and no ultimate revelation of the truth. Everything turned out to be a matter of perspective. Science, history and all systems of knowledge are only socially sanctioned narrations and different forms of storytelling and fiction.

In Nietzschean spirit, Foucault spoke and wrote voluminously about the problematic pursuit of knowledge and how it is related to acquisition and maintenance of power. He argued that all knowledge systems, including the so-called absolute and universal knowledge (of human nature and behaviour i.e. immutable, unchangeable), are not only contingent (dependent on or conditioned by several factors) but also exclude, repress and mask reality. Derrida, who played a major role in uncovering the false dichotomies inherent in philosophical thinking, agreed with Foucault when he said that there was a close relationship between the metaphysical quest for absolute knowledge and political totalitarianism.

In short, Derrida, Foucault and other postmodernists found that the problem, or rather, the source of mischief, whether in science, philosophy or theology, is the idea of a centre—or an origin, truth, essence, god, presence. And the tricky nature of any kind of centre is that it attempts to exclude, repress or marginalise everything else. The idea of centre inevitably spawns opposites: man–woman, inside–outside, rational–irrational, good–evil, body–soul and so on. When thinking in such almost irreconcilable binaries, we tend to privilege one and disregard the other.

Further, the postmodernists tried to show that language does not merely report, represent and describe the world. Rather, language creates the world. Earlier philosophies had taken language for granted and looked at it as a representation of a world that has been handed to us and had no role in the creation of that world. And suddenly now, language was found to be the source of all troubles, which does not so much represent reality as it creates, distorts, discloses, hides and oppresses realities, and is anchored in power, prejudice and ideology. Therefore, languages, not humans, were seen as agents of history.

Even the idea of self, which includes the body, is a result of the growth of language. It is through language that man constructs himself as a subject, and establishes the concept of self or ego.

What then is reality? What is the truth? Simply put, all notions of reality and truth, including the self, are effects of language, that actually lie scattered in bits and pieces, struggling to become round, whole and powerful.

Postmodernism, especially deconstructionism, rendered a devastating blow to various philosophies that claimed universality and infallibility. The purpose of the pursuit of knowledge was suspect and needed to be critically examined, for all texts or philosophies that claimed to have supreme knowledge were found to be full of internal tensions and contradictions and, in fact, defeated their stated goals and claim to truth.

Many philosophers, especially the ones more aligned towards Marxism, such as Hans-Georg Gadamer and Jürgen Habermas, found postmodernism (philosophy represented by the likes of Deleuze, Derrida, Foucault and so on) hugely problematic, quite nihilistic, narcissistic, and thus, unacceptable, since it was seen to devalue the history of emancipatory culture and politics and liberation spirituality.

Hence, the emergence of the critical theory. The Marxism-inspired movement worked towards emancipation from all forms of slavery, be it intellectual, social, cultural and political, in order to create a world that satisfies the needs of people. There are, of course, many different critical theories related to racism, sexism, colonialism and so on—all in the interest of emancipation. But then there is nothing entirely new about these theories which expose oppressive elements of various beliefs and practices.

It seems the pursuit of social and political knowledge has reached a dead end and so philosophers today—hoping to find alternatives to critical theories or to discover new perspectives of understanding reality—have been trying to model their inquiry on sciences, such as physics, biology and psychology. The Western philosophy is once again under critical scrutiny. And the project of knowledge remains an unfinished journey.

However, three things can be considered as the most significant features of Western philosophy. One, scepticism as a method of inquiry led to the development of different schools of thought and various sciences. The empirical approach to test the validity of knowledge has been one of the reasons for the jump in innovation. Two, the idea of justice that has led to the spread of legal philosophy the world over. Three, the idea of salvation, derived from the Christian beliefs of sin, redemption and forgiveness, was transformed into a secular idea of rescuing humankind through progress, reason and justice.

It would be wrong to belittle the pursuit of knowledge, to doubt the sincerity of the philosophers' search for truth or to say that knowledge has not helped humanity at all. It has certainly changed us. But despite how far we have come, if Socrates were still around, he would probably be shocked that humans have remained pretty much the same. There hasn't been much change in the way we think and behave. Jealousy, fear, greed, hatred, pain and stupidity are still some of our most powerful characteristics.

Perhaps it is time for us to admit that in a deeper sense, knowledge has not helped us. Throughout history, human advancement in knowledge has coincided with vaulting ambition, extreme anxieties, wars, genocides and ecological devastation. Knowledge has become mere ideology.

Immanuel Kant proposed the enlightenment project for the progress of humankind based on the values of reason and justice. It was a secular version of the Christian belief in salvation. The project, however, was an illusion. As John Gray, a noted yet controversial philosopher today, said, 'In science, the growth of knowledge is cumulative. But human life as a whole is not a cumulative activity; what is gained in one generation may be lost in the next. In science, knowledge is an unmixed god; in ethics and politics it is bad as well as good. Science increases human power—and magnifies the flaws in human nature. It enables us to live longer and have higher living standards than in the past. At the same time it allows us to wreak destruction—on each other and the Earth—on a larger scale than ever before . . . The idea of progress rests on the belief that the growth of knowledge and the advance of the species go together—if not now, then in the long run. Knowledge does not make us free. It leaves us as we have always been, prey to every kind of folly.'

The advancement of knowledge, science and technology, and the acquisition of power that comes from politics and weapons deludes us into thinking that we are the masters of our destiny. But nature has its own logic and brings about changes that we least expect. We write our history books after events have occurred, trying to fit them neatly into the frameworks of our ideas and beliefs, and presume that we have understood all that needs to be understood. But in actuality, we do not know that we are out of tune with life and lack the grace and honesty to accept that the human condition remains as it was a few thousand years ago.

We are captive to dogmatic discourses and narratives that have brought us to the brink of disaster. Perhaps it is possible to release ourselves from the stranglehold of our ideological prisons. For that, we need to pause. It is not possible to see anything clearly when looking out through the window of a speeding train. We need to slow down. The purpose of knowledge and philosophy is not to change the world but, as the Buddha said, to see it rightly. That is when we will know what has to be done. But first, we need to shed the heavy baggage of ideas that we carry with us, so we may see the world without prejudices.

In Indian spiritual traditions, seeing is considered jnana. It is not knowledge in the conventional sense of the term but a holistic comprehension of reality with your entire being. It is like fire, which can be felt, seen and experienced without needing to name it.

If Western philosophy is like a huge library building with several corridors you walk through to understand the complete range of Western thought, starting from Socrates, Descartes, Derrida, right up to Gray, Indian philosophy is like a big open bazaar where you can wander through and pick your choice: Kapila, Patanjali, the Buddha, Abhinavagupta, Lalleshwari, Kabir, Guru Nanak, Bulleh Shah, Vivekananda, Aurobindo, Gandhi, Ambedkar and many more. The educational walk perhaps finishes with the realisation that all ideas and beliefs have only relative, functional value, and what cannot be understood or known with words must be left alone.

The beginning of the Indian adventure in consciousness can be traced to the Vedas. But there were a few philosophers who preceded the Vedic seers. For instance, Kapila, who, between 600 to 700 BCE, tried to find answers to perennial questions such as: what is the origin of life and the universe? Does god exist? Why is there suffering? Can there be an end to it?

Kapila sutras, or aphorisms, that later came to be called Sankhya philosophy, marked a major departure from god-centred religious conviction by bringing in ideas of evolution and involution in place of creation and destruction. He proposed the concepts of prakriti, the primordial force out of which the universe in all its diversity evolves, and purusha, the spiritual principle or intelligence that powers prakriti to unfold and evolve in its varied forms, almost similar to yin and yang of Taoism, to explain the origin and nature of the universe and life.

According to Kapila, it is not god but prakriti that is the material cause of existence; yet, cause and effect are not entirely separate from each other; in fact, effect is already always there in a potential form in its cause. But then, prakriti by itself is inactive; it is purusha, the spiritual principle, that triggers prakriti to evolve into its varied physical and psychological forms. And, ultimately, Kapila declared that human liberation from conflict and suffering happens through the right knowledge, jnana or *vivekakhyati*, when the individual is released from karma and realises the pristine purity of purusha.

Kapila's twin concepts of prakriti and purusha, along with his *pramanas*, or valid sources of jnana, significantly influenced the development of Indian philosophy. The Sankhya philosophy was one of the earlier schools of thought among the six darshans (which means to see, to experience) alongside yoga—a philosophy combining Sankhya theory with the discipline of meditation; Nyaya—a school of thought based on logic with an emphasis on realism; Vaishesika—an empiricist school of atomism and naturalism; Mimamsa—a philosophy based on faith, and religious disciplines; Vedanta—a philosophy based on non-dualism; Ajivaka—an ascetic sect that believes that things happen as per cosmic principles and not according to free will; and Charvaka—also called Lokayata, a school of philosophy that was atheistic and materialistic—all of which have shaped the Indian philosophy.

The claim that the Vedas are the only source of valid knowledge is not true. The belief that Vedas constitute not *smriti* (what is remembered) but *sruti* (what is heard) and that it is impersonal, authorless and not of human but divine origin, was an invention of Brahminism. Perhaps, it is not strange to attribute a divine origin to certain scriptures because of the limited knowledge people possessed at the time they were written. But the belief came handy for a certain class of people to wield power over others.

In any case, the Vedic mantras and gods found no mention in the Upanishads because of the realisation that liberation, if it even exists, cannot possibly be attained through rituals. To know about the mysteries of the universe, one has to begin with one's self and delve deep within. That is how the Upanishadic quest for truth began. In a sense, the seers of the Upanishads were rebels; they turned away from family, community and even the gods, looking inwards instead.

We do not actually know the authors of the Upanishads, but their texts contain a wide array of ideas and deep philosophy. They include notions of samsara, karma, dharma, moksha and a vision of an interconnected universe with a single, unifying principle behind its diversity—Brahman. Also theories about consciousness, such as the waking state, dream state, dreamless, deep sleep state and finally *turiya*, the state of unitary consciousness—all these ideas and philosophies have had a tremendous impact on Indian thought.

In the sixth century CE, Adi Sankara developed his philosophy of Advaita Vedanta on the Upanishadic ideas of Brahman and atman. He also proposed two kinds of truth:

vyvaharika satya (phenomenal reality) and *paramarthika satya* (ultimate reality). Brahman is the absolute, ultimate reality. It is the infinite being and consciousness, without form, qualities or attributes. It is the ultimate truth—beyond the senses, mind and imagination. From the Brahman's point of view, Sankara asserted, the material world's distinctness and the individuality of the living creatures are all maya—a mere illusion.

The Hindu concept of turiya as the fourth state of consciousness and the Buddhist notion of sunyata, or emptiness, have arguably been the greatest contributions to the field of philosophy. But the world of Western philosophy is yet to reckon with either of them.

The Mandukya Upanishad describes turiya as a state beyond the senses, mind, intellect and even the atman. It is a state of consciousness where even the awareness of the world and of its multiplicity is completely absent, which is referred to as samadhi. Descartes's exultant declaration, 'I think, therefore I am,' was supposedly an assertion of the knowledge that I/you exist. But in the state of turiya, there is no one around to say that I exist; as such, the concept of 'I' is silent and only consciousness or pure awareness exists.

The English words such as 'trance', 'rapture' and 'ecstasy', often used by religious scholars to describe the high mystical state of being, doesn't come close to describing turiya. The fourth state of consciousness, where there is no dreaming, no self-reflection and no operation of will and experience, does not exist in Freudian psychology. In Indian philosophy and spiritual traditions, however, turiya is a much-discussed subject. It is also sometimes referred to as *nirvikalpa samadhi* or *shaja samadhi*; in Jainism as *kaivalya*; and in Buddhism as nirvana or *sunyata*. In modern times, Ramana Maharishi called it *turiyatita*. Philosopher U.G. Krishnamurti called turiya as the state of not knowing, where the mind is in a 'declutched state'.

The exact definition of the notion of sunyata or emptiness may vary within the different schools of Buddhist thought. However, it is central to the Madhyamika philosophy, founded by Nagarjuna. Although the Buddha used the term in his analysis and description of reality, the self and the state of Buddha nature, it was Nagarjuna (ca. 200 CE) who developed it into an entire philosophy. He deployed sunyata in his technique of four-corner negation to point out the illusory nature of our phenomenal experience. By doing so, he exposed the limits of epistemology and demonstrated the futility of all attempts to know what cannot be known.

Nagarjuna's main concern was to prove the fallacy of clinging to views, however profound they may be, and to let go of all our concepts, for all of our knowledge and experience is nothing but a mix of interdependent concepts. They have no *svabhava*, essence, of their own. Nothing exists by itself or in itself. Therefore, to assume that all things and events are self-contained is a fundamental error. It is this ignorance that is the basis for any sort of attachment—whether it is to the self, to people or to things and beliefs. It can only result in a state of sadness, dukkha. There is nothing outside of the conditioned physical and mental elements that constitute our being. There are only views that can neither be affirmed nor denied. They cannot be proven to be true or false. There is neither life nor death, neither joy nor sorrow, neither bondage nor liberation, neither fullness nor emptiness. There is a word in Sanskrit to describe this condition perfectly—*advaya*.

Advaya is non-dual—something without a second. So to even say that *all is one* would imply there is two or more. Hence, when the Buddha was questioned about the nature of life and existence, he simply maintained silence, or smiled. The silence or smile did not indicate 'nothingness'. It meant thought-free wakefulness.

In twelfth-century Karnataka, the mystic-poet Allama Prabhu, expressed it through his poem thus:

> If there is no desire,
> there is no imagination;
> if there is no imagination,
> there is no thinking;
> if there is no thinking,
> there is no Lord of Caves;
> if there is no Lord of Caves,
> there is no truth,
> no void, either.

Buddhists rejected the Hindu idea of Brahman and atman. Much before the postmodern deconstructionists sought to expose and then subvert the various oppositions in philosphical texts and discourses, the Buddhists had maintained that the world, the self and our experience of everything is a product of *vikalpa*, imagination. In other words, with the birth of the mind and the self, the wheel of life, *bhavachakra*—the play of emotions and the cycles of births and deaths—is set in motion. In actuality, it means the birth and continuity of the mind, the thinking-feeling subject, namely, the self.

Adi Sankara and other believers of Advaita Vedanta more or less agreed with the Buddhists—that all ideas and experiences, including of god, are projections of the mind. In fact, they introduced the notion of maya, illusion. This means that birth and death, joys and sorrows, gods and goals and liberation from all such binaries as well, are all tricks the mind plays on us. However, they appear real because of ignorance and the disconnect the self has from the totality of life.

Jainism propagates ahimsa as the *paramo-dharma*, that non-violence is the highest moral virtue. That is Jainism's greatest teaching. Hinduism speaks of the same idea, but ahimsa is not without riders here. Bhishma, dying on a bed of arrows on the battlefield, proclaims ahimsa as the greatest sacrifice. Yet in the Mahabharata and the Ramayana, violence committed for the sake of dharma, in self-defence or for the defence of family, kith and kin is justified. Jainism doesn't allow for such ifs and buts. There, ahimsa is a strict code of conduct. It cannot be justified under any circumstances. All life is considered sacred and has the right to live. So humans cannot hurt other people, animals, plants and even micro-organisms.

Gandhi turned this supreme moral virtue into a weapon to fight British rule. Jainism's determination to follow the path of ahimsa and Gandhi's satyagraha are two great Indian contributions to the world of thought.

Indian philosophies have always been about freedom from conflict and sorrow, and liberation from the divided self into a state of unitary being. Samsara can never be free of violence and pain; we can, at best, work towards creating a society where people are encouraged to follow the path of dharma. Partaking in the right knowledge and conducting ourselves in the correct manner will hopefully allow us to shed our attachments. Or we can surrender our will to our preferred god or deity, bringing all anxieties, fears and sorrows to an end. Or people can step out of the river of samsara, get rid of all their beliefs and attain freedom here and now.

It would be easy to think that the Indian way of life—with the great knowledge it holds and the possibility for humans to reach a higher state of being—is qualitatively different from the life lived in other parts of the world. But that would be a mistake.

While Indians are taught that all life forms, including humans, are connected and goddesses are worshipped as creative, sustaining forces of the universe, the treatment of women and transgenders in this country is cruel and deplorable. The heartless caste system with its graded inequality has resulted in Dalits being seen as less than human.

Jiddu Krishnamurti, the modern mystic-philosopher from India who grew to be one of the radical thinkers of the world, dared to hold up a mirror to Indians and tell them that their claim to a rich, superior spiritual heritage counted for nothing. He was a revolutionary man. He gave up the role of 'world teacher' and walked out of the theosophical society when he realised that neither a guru nor an organisation is required to attain freedom. He questioned, and then rejected established, sacred beliefs as well as the authority of the religious traditions of the East and West.

He also criticised the central ideas and symbols of Vedanta, causing quite a commotion. While assessing scriptural utterances such as 'Prajnanam Brahma,' (Consciousness is infinite), 'Aham Brahmasmi,' (I am that infinite) and 'Tat tvam-asi,' (Thou art that), he also questioned, 'Why do we always attach ourselves to something which is supposed to be the highest? Why not say: I am the river, I am the poor man? Can a conditioned mind that is small, petty, narrow, living on superficial entertainments, can that know or conceive, or understand, or feel or observe the unconditioned?'

What does Vedanta mean? The end of knowledge. If so, Krishnamurti asked, 'Then why should I go through all the labourious process of acquiring knowledge, and then discarding it? Why should not I, from the very beginning, see what knowledge is and discard it? . . . Why did the traditionalists, the professionals, the scriptures, the spiritual leaders not see this? Was it because authority was tremendously important—the authority of the scriptures? Why? Why did they not see this?'

His was an utterly new voice that set a new path to the quest for truth when he declared, 'Truth is a pathless land. Man cannot come to it through any organisation, through any creed, through any dogma, priest or ritual, not through any philosophical knowledge or psychological technique.'

Then came U.G. Krishnamurti, twenty years younger to Jiddu, and like the proverbial disciple, he moved beyond his teacher. His subversive statements touched a raw nerve, undermined our pet beliefs and knocked grand narratives and systems of knowledge off their pedestals. His declarations offered not only release from the tyranny of sacred symbols, ideas, gods and goals but also tendered a foretaste of the vast emptiness. Here are some examples: 'Love is war. Man is memory. Charity is vulgar. Thought is bourgeois. Religions have promised roses but you end up with only thorns. Going to the pub or the temple is the same; it is quick fix. As long as you are searching for happiness, you will remain unhappy. You are not one thing and life another. It is one unitary movement. Messiahs have only created a mess in the world. By using the models of Jesus, Buddha, or Krishna we have destroyed the possibility of nature throwing up unique individuals. Those who recommend that you forget your own natural uniqueness and be like someone else, no matter how saintly that person may be, is putting you on the wrong track.'

His anti-philosophy led many, including the media, to dub him the Reluctant Messiah, the Sage in Rage, the Cosmic Naxalite, the Anti-Guru and so on. But in actuality, paradoxical as it may sound, he marked both a creative continuity of Indian philosophy and a radical departure from it as well. U.G. took forward Indian beliefs in the sense that, in him, there was something of a Nagarjuna, the anti-philosopher of the second century CE; a Gaudapada, the mystic philosopher of the fifth century CE; and an Allama Prabhu, the twelfth-century mystic-poet. They all represented a stream of thought where philosophical structures, including religious discourses and political ideologies, are rejected as inventions which, far from leading humanity to freedom, joy and peace, only create conflict within societies.

U.G. also, however, marked a radical departure from traditional Indian philosophy, especially the Indian enlightenment traditions. He demystified the notion of freedom or enlightenment and redefined it as the natural state in physical and physiological terms. According to U.G., somewhere along the course of evolution, the human species experienced the self or 'I' consciousness. The emergence of the self and the rupture of the human from the unitary movement of life was a simultaneous process. This separation from nature gave man self-consciousness and he accorded himself a position above other species on this planet. And that has been the source of man's many problems.

The self seeks its own continuity. And since it cannot exist forever and has to come to an end, the self creates artificial immortality by way of manufacturing identities, concepts and world views.

U.G. maintained that it is possible to bring the divided self to an end. There is potential to loosen the stranglehold of ideologies that have converted our lives into a battlefield. To do so requires that we stop depending on belief systems for our growth. Once the control that thought has over us ends, the creative energy locked up in our bodies will find release. This transformation of the body–mind is liberation from the prison of ideas and beliefs.

But we do not know how to make it happen. It is said that the lives of sages show us the pathway of transcending the divided self and moving beyond boundaries to live in a state of freedom. More and more people from various fields are becoming aware of the imprisoning nature of beliefs and the need to transcend them. The vast majority of us, however, remain trapped in the stories we have created for ourselves. There seems to be no way out, unless a large-scale biological mutation of the body–mind occurs and releases us from the grip of self-destructive tendencies. Or, like D.H. Lawrence's Jesus (in *The Man Who Died*), we become courageous and make an effort to walk away from all grand narratives we have been taught, drop all non-existent gods and learn to live in the vivid awareness of the unity of all life.

Science is progressive, and its sceptical nature helps it to move towards a better understanding of the physical world. In science, it is possible to retire ideas or theories that don't work anymore. But in the world of philosophy and religious beliefs, we find hard resistance, sometimes even violent opposition, to any change, even in the face of new discoveries.

What we know of life and the world is infinitely small. Perhaps we will never know everything about life and it will remain a mystery. That is because our mind is so fragmented that it can never comprehend the totality of life. More importantly, humans are still evolving, which means the knowledge or texts they have created have to change and evolve too.

VI
Selfishness

RICHARD DAWKINS'S BOOK *THE SELFISH GENE* makes for a fascinating read. It is about the genetic evolution of man on earth, of the journey of a selfish gene's passage from the primordial soup to the *Homo sapiens*.

Curiously, what we gather from this book is that every gene is selfish to the core; it seeks only its own survival and continuity. But these cells do not step on each other's toes or cut each other's throats to exist; rather, they cooperate with each other because they know that their survival depends on the others.

A human being is made up of trillions of such self-protective yet empathetic and cooperative cells. Along with them, humans are also endowed with the self or ego, which is a selfish entity. Perhaps without this trait humans wouldn't have survived nature's harsh conditions during the early phases of evolution. The problem is that our situation hasn't radically changed today. The story of the selfishness continues; in fact, it has only become more complex, insidious and dangerous.

The body constantly faces threats from harmful virus and bacteria and injury-causing accidents. The body protects itself against them until it cannot. And when the body dies, the self is deceased too. But the self or ego abhors death, so it has invented medicines and technologies to prolong the body's existence. For without the body, the self has no life.

Along with maintaining the health of the body, the self has other challenges as well. Its separation from nature and the world had led to a sense of lack and fear. To overcome this feeling, the self has developed various forms of desires in the form of faith or belief systems. Do we call that selfishness? Definitely! The desire for security, the need to love and to be loved, the wish to be happy and prolong one's existence are all acts of selfishness. The human life, which includes personal, religious and social aspects, is built on the foundation of self-interest.

Desire and selfishness are two sides of the same coin. We do not breathe, eat, sleep and relieve ourselves for selfless reasons. We do not love and marry and beget children for the sake of the world. Selfishness is shaped by culture but it also has biological roots. Hence, it is pointless to ask if it is wrong to be selfish, because one cannot help but be thus.

Having said that, we need to distinguish between what may be called healthy selfishness and total self-centredness. It is not always easy to know how and when desire turns into greed.

Let us understand the difference between selfishness and self-centredness. Wanting to be happy is natural but seeking happiness only for oneself and turning a blind eye to the suffering of others is self-centredness. Healthy selfishness is the affirmation of one's own uniqueness, growth, joy and freedom.

Therefore, without demonising selfishness, it is important to ask: is it possible to seek one's security, happiness and excellence without destroying the well-being of others, especially since it only results in insecurity and suffering for both? Can we nurture healthy selfishness that is not opposed to cooperation, empathy and compassion?

The thinking that selfishness is sinful has not helped and never will, rather it will only make one suffer guilt about one's desires and joys, denying one's own authentic self. What is important, therefore, is to do the right thing, and in being honest and genuine in whatever one does.

But even with good intentions, it is possible to harm others. By practising self-abnegation, by sacrificing one's own happiness for the sake of others, people may harm themselves. They may also regret their unfulfilled desires and unrealised potential. In contrast, a person who has healthy self-interest, who has tasted joy, dignity and freedom and actualised their potential, will always do the right thing—and, in the process, not hurt others.

Spiritual traditions often talk about the dissolution and transformation of the self. However, these are loaded terms and we have to use them cautiously. The lives of the sages like the Buddha, Jesus or Ramana Maharshi do not indicate selflessness or absence of the self. Without the self or the mind, it is not possible to function in this world. One cannot taste food, cannot find the way back home and cannot engage in a conversation.

What then is the difference between the Buddha or Ramana and others? In the case of the Buddha, the self with all its attachments and aversions that cause conflict and sorrow has undergone change. Egotism, hatred and greed are done with and there is no more pursuit of non-existent goals. In a sense the self has lost its fat, and become light and functional. It is not a state of self-lessness, rather the self comes in when there is a challenge, when there is a need and when the job is done, it is gone—there is no continuity of the self. The same can be said about the lives of saints or prophets as well. Their lives indicate the possibility of transcending self-centeredness, of overcoming the sense of separateness and attaining the unity of being.

Psychologist Abraham Maslow spoke about healthy selfishness, self-actualisation and peak experience. He argued that it is time for a new vocabulary that incorporates the notion of healthy selfishness. We also need to re-examine religious language, especially concepts of selflessness and thoughtlessness, sin and salvation, good and evil, and all other elements that divide life into irreconcilable binaries, falsifying it.

VII
Love

IN THE 1960S AND 1970S, LYRICISTS, MUSICIANS AND singers created some of the most beautiful love songs for Hindi movies. Besides the enchanting play of melody, romance and erotic feelings, in which the whole universe seemed to participate, the most endearing aspect about some of these songs was the sense of wonder and mystery they expressed about love. The wonderment about love sometimes included wonderment about the whole of life in general. In effect, it often took the form of questions that went something like this: what is this life all about? Until yesterday, I did not know you, yet I feel today that I cannot live without you. Who are you? Who am I? What is this irresistible attraction between the two of us? Is this what they call love?

What's more, some of these love songs took the form of bhakti, or devotional songs, that sounded like the cry of the soul seeking union with the beloved to dissolve into oneness. And it comes as no surprise that these love songs expressing romance were filmed in the lap of nature, with flowers blooming across a lush green landscape, or in pouring rain, drenching the lovers and the earth.

Nowadays, love songs may not express a sense of wonder about relationships, least of all the elements of bhakti, but they do express quite candidly the desire for physical pleasure, companionship and union. Some may find this gross but it is a genuine expression of love.

It is interesting to note here that even in bhakti, the cry of the soul is expressed in physical terms. Rather, the physical becomes the heart and soul of the spiritual quest. For instance, Akka Mahadevi, in one of her powerful poems, conflates bodily experience with the transcendental so that the spirit speaks through the flesh: 'The arrow that is shot should penetrate so deeply that even the feathers do not show/ Hug the body of the lord so tightly that the bones must be crushed to crumble/Weld to the divine until the very welding disappears.'

Then again, these days 'love' has become too general a term to express strong feelings. Attraction towards money, power, sports, music and chocolates is also called love. Indeed, love is a multidimensional emotion. Along with parental and sibling love and conjugal love between man and woman, present in movies, literature and life, is the remarkable and bold declaration of love between men, women, non-binary and transgender people.

Conjugal and Transgender Love

Love is one of the primary emotions besides anger, fear, joy and sorrow. It is also a biological and cultural response.

Neurochemicals such as testosterone, oestrogen, dopamine, oxytocin and vasopressin trigger physiological processes that influence the expression of love and many other emotions. Activated by thought, the endocrine glands trigger the chemical process. But the expression of emotion is shaped and strengthened by culture. Depending on your background, you may give an endearing smile and say 'I love you', invite a person for coffee to a restaurant, or offer them chocolates. And if you didn't know how to express it, you may simply point at a tree, a rising moon or a setting sun and exclaim, 'See, how beautiful that is!'

In the case of transgender love, culture works as a repressive and terror-inducing force. The mind may deceive us, and tell lies in hundred crafty ways, but the body speaks only the truth. Despite societal pressure, biological impulse cannot be curbed. In interviews and in their writings, transgenders have spoken about the overwhelming feeling to seek the company and touch of others. It is like the scream of god, perhaps stronger and more authentic than it is in the realm of bhakti. And the trans people realise there is strong expectation from them to deny the most authentic aspects of their personality. The stories of trans people and their untold suffering exposes the cruelty of our cultures and religions, and how little we know about human nature and the ways of life.

Now, there is another side to love that needs to be considered with honesty. Love is considered a positive, life-affirming emotion, but we cannot be blind to the fact that it can be a negative and destructive force as well. As an expression of affection, kindness and concern for others, love undoubtedly makes the world a happy place. But love sometimes also results in self-centredness, vanity, egotism or self-righteousness, along with an overanxious attachment to people, things and ideas.

There is no point in arguing that negative emotions have nothing to do with love, or that 'pure' love is always life-affirming and positive, for that is not how love, as *passion*, operates in reality. When you are in love and loved, life seems wonderful, but when it is denied and you feel separated from everyone, life is miserable. It is a fact that most people will try anything to secure the well-being of those they love, even if it means destroying the happiness and lives of others. For the sake of family, nation, religion, god or a cause they love most, some people will sacrifice anything.

People kill others out of love for an ideology or god and suffer no guilt because doing so for transpersonal ideals and not personal reasons is acceptable. That is how genocides are committed. And such people are treated as heroes and martyrs.

These actions are not the fault of love. But it is certainly the flaw of the self that is made up of both love and hate, empathy and apathy, compassion and revulsion. Is it possible to choose one over the other? It is! But we have not succeeded. We have been unable to overcome a deep flaw in the make-up of our selves.

In the gospel according to Matthew (5:43–48), Jesus Christ says, 'You have heard that it was said, "You shall love your neighbour and hate your enemy." But I say to you, love your enemies and pray for those who persecute you, so that you may be children of your Father in heaven.'

In one of his songs, Purandara Dasa, a fifteenth-century Kannada poet-saint, urges you to 'invite your enemy home and serve him a good meal.'

One can imagine many heads shaking and muttering: 'This is all a little too much to ask. At best I can decide to not curse or harm the person who hates me. But how can you pray for your enemy and invite them for a meal at your home, or love them? That's impossible! It goes against human nature. It's all right for a saint to advocate and practise such behaviour, but I am only human.'

The logic, however, is profoundly simple: loving your parents, spouse, children, friends, neighbours, is not that difficult. The real test of love lies in loving the one who hates you. What is love if it cannot be extended to all, including your so-called enemy? What is love if it is not forgiving and all-embracing?

One of the aspects of Gandhi's principle of non-violence was an all-embracing love. It means recognising the so-called 'evil doer' as your brother and a victim of circumstance, not somebody who is intrinsically a bad person. It was not just a humane method of conflict resolution through dialogue, mutual respect and understanding, it was also, and more importantly, recognition and acceptance of our indubitable mutual dependance, our natural need for mutual love, cooperation, growth and peace.

Love and Sex

After god and politics, sex is a subject that stirs up our deep emotions. Unlike the other two, we find it difficult to be completely open and honest about sex. When it comes to conjugal relationships, can there be love without sex and sex without love? This question can throw us into a mass of contradictory thoughts and feelings.

It is interesting to note that animals face no confusion or uncertainty about love and sex. Animals are known to show intimacy, affection, kindness and caring. And when in heat, they mate and procreate. There is no grey area here.

It's not as simple with us humans. Love and sex are complex matters. Affection and kindness can be genuine as well as insincere. And sometimes they are expressed with either an ulterior motive or without feelings. Perhaps that is why we add the prefix 'pure'—pure kindness, pure affection, pure love—to show its sincerity. Our thoughts make humans complicated. When we feel fearful, insecure and egotistic, love loses its healing and energising qualities and compassionate touch.

Animals mate only when they are in heat and during specific seasons. Male chimpanzees can mate only when the female comes into oestrus, which may last for ten to fourteen days. Male elephants, on the other hand, mate only once a year. What I'm trying to say is that there is a rhythm to the mating behaviour of animals, but for humans there is none. For, as they say, the urge to have sex resides in the head, not in the genitals.

Sex can be a beautiful expression of love and an act of pleasure. In Hinduism, the trimurtis, Brahma, Vishnu and Shiva, are all married and monogamous. They are often depicted with their spouses, namely, Saraswati, Lakshmi and Paravati, respectively. But the much-married Lord Indra is often portrayed as one full of lust for power and an irresistible longing to seduce wives of other men, transgressions for which he is always punished. Shiva performs intense penance, but he falls in love with Parvati when he sees her, and wonders how, despite his long periods of penance, he could be so drawn to her. Even the gods are bound by the law of life. So when life splits itself in two, manifesting itself as male and female, it gives rise to separateness, along with a longing for union. That is why there is the celebrated form of *ardanarishvara*, a union of Shiva and Parvathi, animus and anima, indicating the transcendence of separation.

Krishna is a great lover, and *Gita Govinda*, songs composed by the twelfth-century poet Jayadeva, is a celebration of his love for Radha and the gopis. Yet, in certain narratives, Krishna is described as an eternal brahmachari, while Narada, wanderer of the seven worlds and a storyteller, who boasts of being an undying celibate, is tricked into marriage to experience the joys and sorrows of human existence before he attains enlightenment. The importance of living life in society is further emphasised when a renowned sage who has spent all his life doing penance for moksha is stopped at the gates of heaven. He is sent back to earth to go through the required experience of samsara before he is allowed into heaven.

In certain Tantric traditions of both Hinduism and Buddhism, sex is seen as a source of creative energy that can steer one towards a state of nirvana. At the peak of this tremendous experience, all thoughts accumulated over millions of years of human evolution come to a standstill. This can, through sadhana, lead to an expansion of consciousness and even catapult one into what is called the zero experience, or the primordial awareness of unity.

So, love and sex are like the sea, vast and deep, holding the secret of human existence. One has to dive deep into the water to have a shot at the pearls hiding in there.

Compassion

Compassion, or *anukampa* in Sanskrit, is generally understood as sympathy and empathy for another being. However, its true meaning is 'to shake with', 'to tremble with' or 'to suffer with'. It is the spontaneous response that arises when you encounter another person's suffering, and the whole of your body and mind participate in it. In a way, it occurs deep down within you because you are not separate from others and consider their suffering your own. Organically and spiritually, we are all connected, like the millions of cells in a body. We are all different from each other in unique ways, but not fully separate.

Today, there is plenty of research which tells us that when an animal is injured or killed, other animals and even plants and trees 'shake or tremble' with the 'victim'. Noted biologist Lyall Watson talks about this 'organic connection' in his revealing work *Beyond Supernature: A New Natural History of the Supernatural.* In it, he draws examples from experiments conducted on the 'behaviour' of plants and trees. He shows that when a plant is 'maltreated', plants and trees close to it empathise with it. Injured trees produce tannin—their chemical defence against danger. As this is happening, plants and trees around it enter an empathetic mode within minutes. For instance, when a hook thorn was deliberately thrashed, it was found that another hook thorn around six feet away showed a 42 per cent increase in tannin, while a silver oak ten feet away produced 14 per cent more tannin within an hour. There was no 'root contact' between them, yet they had 'communicated', which reveals that there is an organic connection between all living things.

The neuroscientist V.S. Ramachandran believes that our 'linear thinking seems to be our default mode of thinking about the world', while 'nature is full of non-linear phenomena'. Extending the discussion in neurological terms, he speaks of a special class of cells called 'mirror neurons' that allow human beings to empathise with others. He illustrates the point by discussing a patient named Smith who was undergoing neurosurgery at a hospital.

Smith's scalp was perfused with local anaesthetic and his skull was opened. The surgeon placed an electrode in Smith's anterior cingulate cortex, a region near the front of the brain associated with pain. As predicted, the doctor was able to find a neuron that became active whenever Smith's hand was poked with a needle. What was astonishing, however, was that the same neuron was similarly activated when Smith watched another patient's hand being poked with a needle. Ramachandran writes: 'It is as if the neuron is empathising with another person. A stranger's pain becomes Smith's pain, almost literally. Indian and Buddhist mystics assert that there is no essential difference between self and other, and that true enlightenment comes from compassion that dissolves this barrier. I used to think this was just well-intentioned mumbo-jumbo, but here is a neuron that doesn't know the difference between self and other. Are our brains uniquely hardwired for empathy and compassion?'

It is not just the brain but the whole body that can feel empathy. The secret probably lies in our ductless glands.

There must be other reasons too that we are still unaware of. We are affected by everything happening in the world, even though we may not consciously feel or know it. All existence is one. Compassion is an expression of that oneness, which cannot be experienced when one is full of ego.

VIII
Free Will

THERE IS A STORY ABOUT TWO INDIAN philosophers. One was bearded and the other clean-shaven. They were arguing about the notions of karma and freewill. The bearded man kept saying that a person's karma—consequences determined by one's past and current actions—determines their life. That there is no free will. The clean-shaven man, however, kept arguing that freedom of choice always exists.

They were passing through a field dotted with pools of water from the previous night's rain, when suddenly they paused in their tracks. Two crabs were fighting nearby. Like two wrestlers, they were trying to catch each other with their limbs. It was quite a show!

'And does your theory of karma hold good for them too?' asked the clean-shaven man.

'Why not?' his friend replied tartly. 'Maybe they were human beings in their previous birth and hated each other. And now their karma is making them fight?'

'What if I intervene and separate them?'

'Then that would mean that your karma was and is still tied up with the two crabs.'

The clean-shaven man stared at the other with disbelief and dismay. Then, in a sudden burst of rage, he shouted, 'I hope we'll never meet again.' He quickly turned around and started walking in the opposite direction.

The bearded man screamed back, 'You never know how karma works!'

Free will means the freedom to make choices without being constrained by external agencies. But it is not that simple a concept; in fact, free will is a rather tricky one. That is because you can argue it both ways: that free will exists and we can determine the course of our lives, or that since we have no control over the forces of nature that created us and shaped us, our lives are predetermined, and so the idea of free will is wishful thinking.

However, a large part of Western philosophy and almost all religious discourses or political ideologies work on the assumption that our destiny is in our hands and that we can build a world as per our wishes and ideals. Nietzsche suspected that concealed behind the idea of free will is man's determination to seek power. The idea of free will is a human—indeed, all-too-human—invention, shaped by those in positions of power who, without feeling any personal guilt, judge others as guilty, support punishment, or carry it out themselves.

It seems like a well-thought-out macabre plot. If there is no evil, our belief in god and final judgement become erroneous.

Similarly, if there is no wrong taking place in the world, our legal system, too, is rendered pointless. If a person does something malicious because of causes they have no control over, then who is to be blamed and punished? In short, if humans have no control over what has happened in the past, they cannot have control over its consequences.

That would be more or less the position of the incompatibilists. That is: if the world is causally determined, or determined by the laws of nature (about which we may not have a full and clear understanding), then, since human beings are an integral part of the world, their lives too are determined by the laws of nature. Then the belief that we have a free will, or freedom of action, is an illusion.

On the other hand, compatibilists believe there is a difference between freedom of will and freedom of action. For example, one may have several evil thoughts but they decide whether they want to act on them or not. This means that a person has the power to make rational decisions, therefore, individuals are morally responsible for their actions.

There are different shades of compatibilism and incompatibilism, but we'll not go into that here. However, both these positions exist and it is perfectly possible for individuals in different life situations to swing between them, although it must be said that generally humans have a strong, almost instinctive, sense of freedom.

Today, most of the critical writings on the subject of consciousness, and on the nature and functioning of the mind in particular, suggest that our experience of free will is an illusion. In line with Nietzsche's position that a great part of our activity remains unconscious, present-day discussions maintain that we generally think we are doing things out of choice, when in fact we are not. The unconscious—a mechanism that is unfathomable—creates both the conscious thought about an action and the action itself, and produces the feeling that the action has emanated out of our choice or free will. As social psychologist D.M. Wegner said, 'So, while our thoughts may have deep, important and unconscious causal connections to our actions, the experience of conscious will arise from a process that interprets these connections, not from the connections themselves.'

This position seems to fly in the face of common sense that we are the agents of our actions, that out of our thought-feeling, we consciously initiate actions. But that is an illusion. It is the self that creates this illusion and seeks continuity by thinking it is independent and free of all external agencies when in actuality, it is not.

But what is this self? It is an artificially created entity that identifies itself with emotions, memories, conscious and unconscious drives and propensities. In Indian philosophy, this is referred to as samskaras or *vasanas*. How it all plays out depends on the person's background, culture, religion and politics.

The idea that life is a play and the self is illusory have been central to the philosophies of both Hinduism, Buddhism and other enlightenment traditions for more than 2,000 years now. This may be analysed in two ways.

One, for all appearances, the human mind, the ego, is the creation of past and present karma, influenced by vasanas, which are mental dispositions or tendencies. The self is the thinker and doer, its actions, while emanating from past karma, also gather fresh karma that become the cause of future life. Hence the existence of samsara, cycles of birth and death. But if a person seeks joy, peace and ultimate freedom, then, by exercising one's will, acquiring jnana and performing good karma, one creates the possibility for a happy life, and can finally achieve liberation from samsara.

Two, the ego or self, including a person's will, is a conditioned phenomenon. The 'I' or the self is the coordinator of thoughts. It links up all thoughts into a narrative, which itself is an illusion. This is because thoughts exist, not the thinker. The thinker is an artificially constructed entity. So, freedom would mean not free will but independence from, or transcendence of will, which is the self—the movement of desire and fear, joy and sorrow. Therefore, it follows that those who are free, unattached to ideas and beliefs, do not act as per their will, but live and move in tune with the flow of life. There is no thinker, but only thought; no actor, but only actions, and their inescapable consequences.

IX
Fear

It is believed that children who are six to eight months old express no fear. It is only when they grow older that they slowly develop a sense of what is safe and what is harmful. This does not apply to all children because there have been cases of three-year-old kids expressing no fear. This is not because the amygdala in the brain—which identifies what is harmful and not—is not fully developed yet. It could be because the sense of separateness from the world has not been developed yet.

Our bodies are amazing. Through the release of hormones, the endocrine system regulates our bodily functions such as metabolism, sexual desire, reproduction and sleeping and waking cycles. The job of the thymus gland is to make white blood cells that fight infection and develop the immune system as a child matures. According to the medical science, although some T-cell development (that fights infection) continues throughout adult life, the thymus starts to shrink in size after puberty, becomes less active as one gets older and then stops functioning completely in old age.

Interestingly, in spiritual literature of Indian yoga, and records of ancient Chinese, Egyptian and Mayan civilisations, the thymus gland, located in the upper part of the chest behind the sternum and in front of the heart, is associated with affable emotions such as forgiveness, love and compassion. According to Kundalini yoga, the *anahata* chakra, which is located at the exact spot of the thymus, when activated, enables a person to feel one with the world. The life experiences of sages such as Anandamayi Ma, Ramana Maharshi, the Mother of Pondicherry and U.G. Krishnamurti offer enough evidence of the crucial role the thymus plays in the transcendence of separateness and of coming to the state of unitary experience.

I talk about the thymus here to suggest that fear, especially psychological fear, is linked to the increasing sense of separateness from the world. This is probably connected to the shrinking of the thymus as we become adults. The more we feel a sense of separateness, the lonelier and more fearful we become.

Let us distinguish between physical or instinctual fear, which we share with the animal family, and psychological fear, which is peculiar to human beings. The fear of threat to one's physical existence, are all conditioned, natural fears. We can also call them survival instincts, which trigger a set of physiological changes that help us to respond and act skilfully. There isn't much we can do about them; they are like natural alarm systems that are essential for our protection. For instance, when we see a snake, we instinctively run in the opposite direction. This happens without the exercise of our will or thought.

Psychological fear is not based on instinct. It is a cultivated feeling maintained by the self or ego for its survival. It mimics physical fear because both cause symptoms like shortness of breath, dizziness, sweating, hot or cold flushes and so on. However, while physical fear does protect humans, psychological fear can *never* protect the self or the ego from injury, insecurity and the dread of extinction.

Psychological fears take many forms: fear of death, fear of god and punishment, fear of failure and the future, fear of authority of gurus, fear of insecurity, fear of police and penalty, fear of losing what you have and of not getting what you want. From the time it emerged, the self or ego lives in fear. There is no freedom from the suffering brought on by it because it is in the very nature of the self to forever feel insecure.

From the perspective of deep spirituality, perhaps even of depth psychology, experience springs from dread. Happiness is also a kind of fear, for when we experience it, we are afraid of losing it. In fact, strange as it may sound, fear is at the core of every experience and it takes on different avatars such as likes and dislikes, joy and sorrow, and search for security, knowledge, power and truth. In effect, fear is the offspring of duality. If there is no separation, there is no samsara, no search, no experience, whether pain or pleasure, joy or sorrow, and there is *no fear at all.*

'Abhayam Brahman (fearlessness is Brahman),' declares the Brihadaranyaka Upanishad. It means freedom not from physical fears or phobias but from psychological worries. It is possible. And once you are free of such fears, you go with the flow of life, and you are, to borrow a phrase from D.H. Lawrence, 'breast to breast with the cosmos' and with the vivid awareness of the oneness of life.

X
Freedom

THE POPULAR POEM *MENDING WALL* BY AMERICAN poet Robert Frost is a good place to start talking about freedom. In the very first line of the poem, you read:

> Something there is that doesn't love a wall

Then, somewhere in the middle, it is repeated:

> Something there is that doesn't love a wall, that wants it down.

In response to it, his neighbour only mutters what sounds like a wisecrack:

> 'Good fences make good neighbours.'

Indeed, human beings love to make boundaries, and break them too. In Sri Aurobindo's words, 'The whole world yearns after freedom, yet each creature is in love with his chains; this is the first paradox and inextricable knot of our nature.'

Boundaries, nationalities, religions and languages serve to both unite and separate people. Yet we want to break down the walls, reject borders, discard beliefs and ideas that restrict us and fly freely like birds.

According to Karl Marx, freedom meant liberation from the structures of a capitalist system, which is responsible for human oppression, exploitation and alienation. And to him, freedom was a collective or a social thing, primarily of economic nature. His theories were oriented towards freeing the masses who were struggling for survival through a proletarian revolution to the 'realm of freedom'. Mikhail Bakunin, a Russian revolutionary anarchist and socialist, was an advocate of individual freedom and critical of Marx's 'authoritarian socialism' and 'dictatorship of the proletariat'. Bakunin had significant influence on the thinkers of his time. Writing about individual freedom in *God and the State*, he described a free person as one who has 'severed every link with the social order and with the entire civilised world; with the laws, good manners, conventions, and morality of that world'. In a sense, Nietzsche, in his philosophical fiction *Thus Spoke Zarathustra*, worked out Bakunin's vision of a free individual through the character of Zarathustra and his ideas of 'overman' and 'superman'.

In India, an *avadhuta*, one who has 'passed away from' or 'shaken off' all worldly attachments and cares, is considered one who has attained individual freedom. The avadhuta has rejected all systems of belief and practice and walks the world with no destination in mind, no purpose of meaning and lives in the bright and lucid non-dual state of freedom.

The avadhuta follows a paramapara, not in the sense of a fixed, institutionalised tradition passed on from generation to generation, or from gurus to disciples. Sometimes, the term 'avadhuta' is used as a generic term to describe all homeless ascetics and yogis who live the life of total renunciation. They are indifferent to the conventions of the 'civilised' world and live as per the diktats of their heart. Sarahapada, Allama Prabhu and Vemana were a few noted avadhutas. It is likely that Bakunin and Nietzsche would not have heard of these avadhutas, and certainly not the two outstanding women mystics of the twelfth and fifteenth centuries, Akka Mahadevi and Lalleshwari, respectively. They rejected their husbands and, to use Bakunin's telling words again, severed 'every link with the social order and with the entire civilised world; with the laws, good manners, conventions, and morality of that world'. They even shed their clothes, walked naked and lived in a state of supreme freedom.

New World, New Human

The idea of 'freedom' is one of multidimensional longing, and so naturally it means different things to different people. It could mean freedom from hunger and poverty for the economically challenged; freedom from coercion, discrimination, oppression and fear for minorities, and freedom from all forms of social restrictions for radical activists, anarchists and spiritual revolutionaries.

The words 'rebellion', 'revolt', 'uprising', 'disobedience', 'non-cooperation', 'defiance' and many more indicate the human struggle for liberty, autonomy, self-determination and choice. What's ironical is that humans themselves create oppressive conditions, and rebel against them as well.

Almost all political and social revolutionary movements have arisen from grand ideas of freedom, liberation, empowerment, ideas of the New World, New Man, New Order and then, in course of time, turned intolerant of other views, leading to wars, genocides and tyrannies. It is in fact the story of imperialism, Nazism, Bolshevism, Islamism (of the Jihadi type), Zionism, Crusades and Hindu nationalism. Human history is a catalogue of oppression and revolt, bondage and liberation, despair and hope, conflict and violence. The realisation of the kingdom of god on earth, of the stateless state, of an egalitarian society, remains a dream. The fight for political, social, economic and individual freedom remains an ongoing struggle.

It would, of course, be wrong to say that no good has come from these movements, that human life is the same as it was thousands of years ago or that humankind has not seen any progress.

Movements against discrimination based on race, colour, religion; movements in favour of gender equality, transgender rights; human rights and civil rights movements in support of the dignity and freedom of black people, Dalits and so on, have vastly improved the human condition. Human culture has indeed changed by leaps and bounds, but *human nature*, with immense capacity for both good and bad, remains unaffected. As the walls of separation, discrimination and injustice continue to fall, new walls of separation, inequity, bigotry and intolerance keep getting built, resulting in conflict, suffering and death.

Spiritual Freedom

Religion is bondage. You can be born a Hindu or Christian or Muslim or Jew even before you learn to walk and begin to speak and, one day, die as a member of that religion. Salvation can happen only within the framework of your belief system. If you are a believer, you go to another world or heaven and enjoy eternal bliss; otherwise, you are banished to the eternal torments of hell. Religion has set up many such walls to keep its followers in a state of fear and insecurity, even as believers think that these boundaries keep them secure.

In contrast to religion, spirituality is a deep yearning to bring down these walls. It has to be distinguished from politics, even religion, even though some people believe that spirituality is at core of every religion.

The state of being where there is no separation, no conflict or sorrow, is considered as nirvana in Buddhism and *jeevanmukti* in Hinduism. If release from the culturally conditioned and divided nature of our being is not possible, then our search for freedom would be futile, and we will be stuck in the mire of conflict forever. Freedom from fear and sorrow is possible. The lives of the sages and mystics of all religions are proof of that. We know it is possible to end suffering; otherwise we wouldn't be asking questions, searching for answers and looking for freedom.

In reality, we cannot divide or compartmentalise freedom as social, political and spiritual; they all blend into each other. In dire economic situations, you cannot think of freedom, because *annam* is Brahman, food is Brahman. Food and shelter are your pressing needs; and in a socially and politically oppressive society, you are held back from pursuing what you want. There are always exceptions; people who did not care much for external conditions and followed the path they wanted to. In this context, and in the Indian situation in particular, two persons stand out. Sri Aurobindo and Gandhi's lives were dedicated to the attainment of holistic freedom.

At one time a radical political activist, Aurobindo turned to spirituality in his later years. To him, freedom was both collective and individual in nature. In a sense, he gave a political turn to spirituality, which was till then predominantly seen as a purely personal endeavour. Almost in the style of Marx, he spoke about the god experiences of sages and mystics and how it was time to now transform humans into supramental beings and thus create a new world.

According to Aurobindo, spirituality was at best a great romance, not a deep love. It was not good enough to bring about a 'terrestrial realisation' or evolution. He had no doubt that nature was pushing humankind towards the creation of a new species on earth that would live and flourish in the realm of freedom. But humans in their present condition were not capable of ushering in such a radical change. Altering political philosophies or changing human institutions would not help either. There must be another way, he argued, a way that would not only resist but also overcome the downward pull of the divided self.

Aurobindo's integral yoga philosophy was aimed at going beyond the mind and the overmind, which, he believed, can at best create mystics, sages, great scientists and leaders. There was certainly more to nature's design, to this cosmic play. To rephrase his words, nature is seeking to evolve beyond the mind. If the animal is a living laboratory in which nature has worked out the human, the human may well be a thinking and living laboratory in whom and with the conscious cooperation of which nature creates a new species that is free from the ills of the present age.

Gandhi, on the other hand, was a peculiar combination of an idealist and a pragmatist, and a spiritual empiricist of sorts. According to him, a genuine quest for and the realisation of truth and freedom is possible only within society. His philosophy of ahimsa or non-violence was not just about refusing to hurt people but about *engagement* with the world to free society from all forms of violence. Ahimsa is a non-violent approach to resolve a conflict because it can keep alive the creative possibilities of dialogues along with the plural ways of knowing and being. Finally, the practice of ahimsa entails liberation from not only historical, political and social oppression and injustice but also individual freedom.

Ambedkar, too, adopted a non-violent form of protest, and a constitutional approach to resolving conflicts in society and fighting for the rights and freedom of Dalits. American civil rights activist Martin Luther King Jr was similarly inspired by the teachings of Jesus and influenced by Gandhi's non-violent fight against British rule, and adopted Gandhi's method of non-violence to fight racism.

In fact, across centuries, individuals, including women, Dalits, black people and other marginalised groups, have engaged in fearless non-violent struggles against oppression and injustice by refusing to cooperate with the oppressors and by disobeying authority. But historical accounts have given them little recognition.

XI
Death

ONCE, A SEEKER OF TRUTH ASKED A SAGE, 'SIR, what is death?'

'Are you really serious?' the sage asked. 'But why do you want to know?'

'Sir,' said the seeker, 'Isn't it natural to want to know? I'm terribly curious.'

'All right,' replied the sage. 'But you will have to first die in order to know it.'

The seeker was confused. Surely there was no coming back after death, so how could one know what death is? How would he learn if there was life after death? Or did the sage mean that there is no way one could know about death? That it is unknown and will remain unknown? Has anyone come back from death and talked about it?

Death as a Passage to the Other World

The story goes that after being protected from the vicissitudes of life for a long time in his palace, when the Buddha went out into the world, he was shocked to discover that humans suffered illnesses, old age and death. This experience is believed to have set him on a quest for the truth and the end of sorrow. Today, there is no such protection from the harsh realities of life; in fact, we are bombarded by news of human suffering and death every day. Unlike the Buddha, we are used to suffering and death. We also do not seek the truth, perhaps because we have enough beliefs and ideas about death and life after death that may not end sorrow or reveal the truth, but shield us from dread and spiritual angst. But when one is actually at death's door, one breaks and is at a loss.

One is declared biologically dead when there is no heartbeat and no brain activity. This condition is irreversible. Medical science stops here, and religion takes over.

All religions hold the belief that there is life after death.

Christian Belief

Christians believe that physical death is only a passage to eternal life in another realm, which could either be heaven or hell. After death, it is not just the soul, which is supposed to be non-physical, but also the physical body which when raised by Christ at the end of time (as promised in his Second Coming), enters the other realm.

Death, it is said, was a punishment for the abuse of freedom granted in the Garden of Eden to Adam and Eve. And the idea of death as sin was passed on to their descendants. Thus, death became the universal human fate.

Orthodox Christian traditions, including the Church, may have dropped some aspects of their initial eschatology, but they still maintain that there will be a resurrection of bodies at the end of time, and on Judgement Day, humans shall be sent, in accordance with their beliefs and deeds, to either heaven or hell.

Islamic Belief

Muslims do not believe in the resurrection of bodies; rather, they think that when a human being dies, the soul will enter a state of waiting until Judgement Day. Practising Muslims, who have performed good deeds, will journey to their permanent home in the afterlife, the Garden of Delight, and will be united with their loved ones. Nonbelievers who have veered off the good path will end up in hell, don garments of fire and suffer without relief till eternity.

Special treatment is meted out to jihadis, those who die in the holy war. All their deeds are granted exemption and the mandatory judgement is waived off. They are also immediately ushered into the Garden of Delight to be with their loved ones.

Hindu Belief

Hindus believe that after death you go first to hell to suffer your bad karma, after which you move on to heaven to enjoy your good karma. The more popular belief, however, is that humans undergo cycles of death and rebirth called samsara, and that this will go on till they exhaust all bad karma and attain moksha, or release from this cycle.

Buddhism

We are told that the Buddha did not believe in the idea of a soul. Rather, he refused to get tangled into beliefs about souls and the afterlife. He spoke only about sorrow and the way to end it, and about the state of nirvana, where metaphysical questions about soul, death and the afterlife become irrelevant. However, most Buddhist traditions believe that people go through cycles of birth and death until they attain nirvana. It is believed that the structure of the mind with its bad and good karma survives physical death, and takes on a new life. The state of the mind before death is likely to determine its next life. So, it is crucial to prepare the mind by freeing oneself of attachments, aversions and fear through meditation, before life-breath, the prana, departs.

Sallekhana: Voluntary Death through Fasting

According to Jain philosophy, everything in the world is made up of matter, except souls (jivas) and space. Even karma is matter, and samsara is the entanglement of jiva in matter (*ajiva*). The liberation of jiva from ajiva is nirvana, which can be realised first by shedding karma gradually, and then by absolute withdrawal from outward life. This results in a fast unto death called *sallekhana*. Sallekhana, also known as *samadhi-marana*, literally means to 'scour out' passions and the body by gradually abstaining from food and drink. Since it is not an act of passion, and one does not employ poisons or weapons to die, sallekhana is not considered suicide. It is better, say Jains, to mortify the flesh and end oneself so as to not harm or kill any other living thing.

Sallekhana is observed by both ascetics and laypeople, including men and women of all economic classes.

There are many similar methods of religious deaths practised in both Buddhism and Hinduism. They are undertaken by first slowing down and then completely stopping consumption of food and drink, by walking into a river and drowning (*jala-samadhi*) or by seeking an underground burial (*bhoo-samadhi*). According to tradition, after a saint completes their mission in life, they cease the functions of the body voluntarily by uniting the mind with god. The body is then buried. And it is believed that the place around a jiva-samadhi has very high spiritual magnetic force. Almost all the Siddhars of Tamil Nadu are said to have entered into jiva-samadhis. Guru Raghavendra Swami's jiva-samadhi site at Mantralaya in Karnataka is a popular place of pilgrimage.

Near-Death Experience

Today, the term 'near-death experience' (NDE) refers to a broad range of personal experiences associated with impending death: extreme fear; anguish; distress; intense sensations such as detachment from the body; feelings of levitation; total serenity, security or warmth and so on. NDEs may take place either spontaneously, in certain circumstances or due to factors we know little about. During an NDE, it seems that there is an opening into a different level of consciousness in which a larger reality, transcending time, space and matter, arises. This 'opening' may lead a person to deeper mystical experiences, or to a greater understanding of life with no fear of death. One becomes more spiritual, but not necessarily religious. The person can even lose interest in seeking pleasure or acquiring material wealth, and develop compassion for others. Or all these feelings may disappear completely in due course, with no fundamental change in the person's personality.

Ending the Fear of Death

What I'm about to share here is a real story about someone who was a fairly well-known person in the social circles and the literary world. He was intelligent and wise. Life had treated him well and he had led a good life. He was in his late seventies and dying. The doctors had said that there was no hope. But the man was afraid and did not want to die.

One day, he learnt that his old school friend, K, now a noted spiritual teacher, was in town. He desperately wanted to meet K and asked to meet him.

The next morning, when K came to his place, the man was lying on a cot, surrounded by his wife, children and close relatives. As K walked into the room, the old man waved him to a chair and asked his family to leave them alone for a while.

The dying man looked at his old friend and said with difficulty: 'You know, I have thought about living a great deal, and even more about dying, because I have a protracted illness. Death seems like such a strange thing. I have read various books to deal with this problem, but they were all rather superficial.'

'Aren't all conclusions superficial?' K asked.

'I am not sure,' the old man replied. 'If I could arrive at a satisfying conclusion, that would have some significance for me. What's wrong with that?'

With remarkable tact, K agreed, only to point out that the mind had the power to create every form of illusion, and to be caught in it seemed unnecessary and immature.

But the old man persisted. 'I have lived a fairly rich life, and have followed what I thought to be my duty. But I am human. Anyway, that life is all over now, and here I am, a useless thing. Fortunately, my mind has not been affected. I have read much, and I am still eager to know what happens after death. Do I continue onwards, or is there nothing left when the body dies?'

K asked tenderly, 'Once again, if I may ask, why are you so concerned about what happens after death?'

'Doesn't everyone want to know?'

K said, 'My friend, tell me, if we don't know what living is, can we ever know what death is? It is possible that living and dying are the same thing, and the fact that we have separated them may be the source of our sorrow. Why doesn't one allow the whole ocean of life and death to be?'

There were tears in his eyes as the old man spoke. 'I don't want to die. I have always been afraid of death. I have read so much about death because I want to get rid of this fear. That is why I am begging you to tell me more. You are a great teacher and I have been blessed to be your friend. What you tell me will be true. And this truth will liberate me.'

'But who is this "me"? K asked him. 'The "me" exists only through identification with property, a name, family, failures and successes and all the things you have been and want to be. You are whatever you identify as.'

The dying man was still not ready to let go of the question. He grew desperate. He begged his old friend to be compassionate. Then he cried, 'Are you saying I am beyond all help?'

Even though K sounded merciless, he was being truthful, which *was* an act of compassion. He said, 'The question of help doesn't arise. The very need for help is the problem. It is preventing you from letting all things go. Release all the ideas and beliefs you have gathered over the years. Truth is a strange thing. You cannot capture it nor can you hold it in your thoughts. Realise this and let everything go. You must walk alone on the journey of life and death. You cannot take comfort in knowledge, experience or memories. The mind must be purged of all the things it has gathered in its quest to feel secure. Gods and virtues must be given back to the society that bred them. Perhaps then there is complete freedom.'

XII
Maya

HAVE YOU OBSERVED A SUNRISE? THE SOFT BREEZE that kisses your cheek as the full light is suddenly upon you and the world starts looking sharp. In the evening on a beach, have you studied the waves? Their rise and ebb against the unending horizon and water rushing towards you and around your feet, filling you with indescribable joy. Birds twitter in tree branches and flower buds bloom in the morning light. All these experiences fill you with wonder. But is there a purpose to them? And what does it mean when tsunamis and earthquakes bring down all that is standing?

You have seen infants cry and smile, and gurgle with laughter. They wail when they experience discomfort or hunger, and smile when all is well. Perhaps that is all there is to life. But when there is discomfort or anxiety, we ask questions about life and come up with our own theories about why things happen the way they do.

The seers, renowned for their insights and discourses on life, living and the human condition, which majorly influenced the development of Jainism, Hinduism, Buddhism, Sikhism and other belief systems, were truly clever and wise. From the many texts they left behind, we learn that they dove deep into the matrix of life, and found *nothing*, yet, paradoxical as it may sound, *everything* there. It was full, brimming over with life, yet empty too. Is this reality, which seems true one second, and unreal the next? Then there was utter stillness, when the 'I', the perceiver, went silent. It all seemed a play. A play of perspectives and interpretations. Real yet not true; true yet not real. The seers called it maya.

Maya is a loaded term, with layered meanings. For instance, it refers to the Goddess Maya; the illusory power of Brahman; the mysterious power, wisdom and skills of the gods. In the non-dual schools of thought, especially Advaita Vedanta, Brahman alone is real. Everything else is a fleeting appearance, like a trick at a magic show. That is maya!

Maya is often translated as 'illusion', but that is only partly true. Rather, it means that all views are varying perspectives. If we look deeper, even etymologically speaking, maya means 'to measure'. To measure something, there has to be space, time and a point of reference. The self or the 'I' takes birth in that space–time, and that is the *point*; with reference to this point, the self, we create another point and try to measure it. Anything we measure or experience from that point is subjective. And to think of it in objective, absolute terms would be an illusion.

In other words, everything is *mano-maya*, mind-made. It is a wondrous construct, a make-believe world. Indeed, it is all a *lila*, a play—a tremendous play displaying an apparent beginning and end, life and death, joy and sorrow, fear and bliss—a terrific, relentless movement of life. There is no point in asking why because there is no answer. Nobody has the answer. As Nasadiya Sukta in the Rigveda would say:

> . . . but, after all, who knows, and who can say
> whence it all came, and how creation happened?
> The gods themselves are later than creation,
> so who knows truly whence it has arisen?
> Whence all creation had its origin?

Nobody knows, for it is not in the realm of knowing. Nevertheless, you enjoy and suffer the play as long as you want to be on stage. But once you get off the stage, or get thrown off it, everything changes. And you'll see that it was all an appearance, a marvellous maya. Then if you smile like an infant looking at the world with unblinking eyes, with no questions whirring around in the head, it is maya smiling at herself.

Adi Sankara used the two terms, *vyvaharika satya*, empirical reality, and *paramarthika satya*, ultimate reality, to explain this paradox. It is quite likely that he borrowed from Nagarjuna the two notions of reality: *samvritisatta*, conventional truth employed for a practical purpose, and *paramarthasatta*, supreme truth or the truth of the void. He described Brahman as infinite being, infinite consciousness and infinite bliss—without form, qualities or attributes. In short, it is the 'ultimate truth'. He also asserted that from the point of view of the experience of this ultimate truth, everything else—the material world, its distinctness, the individuality of the living creatures—are all a mere dream, maya.

According to Buddhists, samsara is a product of imagination. With the arising of the mind, the self, samsara and the duality arise. This is the wheel of life. It is also known as bhavachakra: the play of emotions and the cycles of births and deaths. Concepts such as causation, primary elements, personal soul, supreme spirit, sovereign god and creator are all handiworks of the imagination.

Sometimes the world, its aggregates, are described as a lightning flash, a bubble, a white foam on a wave or a thunder cloud. The Mahayana text *Prajnaparamita* that is believed to have perfected the way of seeing the nature of reality points out that dharmas, the five aggregates (form, sensation or feeling, perception, mental activity or formation and discernment) and all other beings, including nirvana, bodhisattvas and buddhas, are like an illusion.

Interestingly, in science, dark matter is believed to account for 85 per cent of the substance in the universe. It is called 'dark' because we do not know how it affects the universe and life. Add to this the theory that what we hear and see is only a fraction of the world. Our eye takes in only 2 per cent of what we see and rest is lost.

If thoughts are a translation of our sensory experiences of the world in the form of meaningful words, then it can perceive only a small part of the world. And we have no clue about how the unknown—unseen dark matter or energy—affects the world and influences our thoughts. If this is true, what is reality?

Again, we do not know. And based on our extremely limited understanding, we have constructed our ideas of the world and life. The suggestion of maya, therefore, makes sense. Our experience or perception of the world is like an illusion or, at best, an incomplete perception.

Absurdism and Maya

In Western philosophy, the idea of the 'absurd' comes close to the idea of maya. But that is, at best, half-baked philosophy. It is certainly an influential point of view, even though it may not carry the different shades and flavours of maya.

According to absurdism, it is futile to search for meaning in an incomprehensible universe that is devoid of it. Absurdism may be seen as the fallout of the tension between the world lacking inherent meaning and the human yearning for purpose.

The idea of absurdism is attributed to Soren Kierkegaard, the nineteenth-century Danish philosopher, and it later developed into a theory by twentieth-century French philosopher and novelist Albert Camus. It would be useful here to consider two other, similarly audacious philosophies: nihilism and existentialism. It wouldn't be incorrect to say that absurdism, nihilism and existentialism are born of the same source: an existential crisis. In different contexts, all three concepts carry varied connotations.

However, nihilism means that all views and values about human existence, morality and meaning are baseless; that is to say there is no god, no heaven or hell, no purpose to human existence, and it is thus pointless to dwell on metaphysical questions. Existentialism is in agreement with nihilism, yet in it is a wilful belief that it is possible to create our own meaning and purpose to life through the choices we make. Absurdism, too, as I said earlier, believes that the universe is irrational and meaningless. But it sidesteps the conflict involved in the other two theories and, unlike existentialism, refuses to invent any meaning for our existence. Instead, it advocates that we accept absurdism as the essential human condition and move on with life. All three streams of thought strongly influenced modern literature and theatre by exploring themes of isolation, loneliness, meaninglessness of life and the laughable search for meaning where none exists.

Maya would readily accept all three positions without demur, but point out that existential crisis and angst are present in the very nature of samsara. Since samsara and its author, the 'I' or the self, spring from divisive consciousness, joy and sorrow, fear and hope are all its different states of being in different situations. However, once you realise that it is absurd to seek an anchor in faith, the search falls by the wayside. With it goes away the attachment to all abstract ideas of life, and you experience a lightness of being. You will play along, free from all delusions.

A story goes that in an open meeting, a seeker asked the Buddha about the nature of reality. Instead of answering the question, the Buddha only twirled a white flower in his fingers and held it before the seeker. Everyone was silent, wondering what the Buddha could be hinting at. Only Mahakasyapa, one of his close disciples, smiled at this revelation.

In the world of maya, absurdity itself is the message. The meaninglessness of life, rather the meaning we put on the movement of life, makes only comical sense. Hence the smile, which expresses the disciple's amusement at his understanding that ultimately, nothing is ever really understood.

Reflections on Some Frequently Asked Questions

What is Normal?

NORMALCY IS A CULTURAL CONCEPT AND ITS meaning keeps changing when new understandings of human nature and progressive values emerge in societies. Talking about the theories and practices in the medical field in particular, Canadian physician, renowned author and speaker Gabor Mate says '. . . our culture's skewed idea of normality is the single biggest impediment to fostering a healthier world.'

The idea of normality has wreaked havoc on human lives. There have been times when killing enemies' children and raping their women was considered normal, slavery was thought of as approved by god and the killing of infant girls endorsed. Men and women who questioned religious authorities or pursued their spiritualities that apparently went against the conventional or institutionalised forms of religion were either burnt at the stake or beheaded in public. Lower caste people who broke caste rules and sought *brahmavidya* (the knowledge and experience of Brahman) or married upper-caste men or women, were punished severely and even put to death.

Today, the progressive view that we need to be tolerant towards non-traditional beliefs and practices, and that values of justice and human rights will usher in an enlightened and healthy society, may be accepted in theory. But on the ground, the idea of 'normality' continues to wreak havoc on our lives. One wonders what would be the fate of the twelfth-century mystic-poet Akka Mahadevi in India today. Akka, which means elder sister, rebelled against all social norms, broke every caste and gender rule, shed her clothes and walked naked in search of her lord, Chennamalikarjuna. She would most likely be called 'crazy' today, and in some orthodox societies, probably be locked up or even stoned to death.

So, once again, what is normal? Are wars in the name of god, nationality, democracy and freedom normal? Are nations that pour billions of dollars to strengthen their armed forces, produce and amass nuclear weapons that can only be used to destroy the world several times over to be considered normal countries? Is income and wealth disparity normal and to be accepted? Is it all right for a country to have 5 per cent of its citizens possess more than 60 per cent of its wealth while a large population lives in dire poverty?

The concept of average may be useful in arithmetic, statistics and a few other disciplines. But the way it has been used in certain fields as an ideal to be pursued has had an unpleasant effect on our social consciousness. For instance, the idea of average height, weight, food consumption, blood pressure, heart rate and so on as normal has skewed our understanding of what constitutes health and well-being. It has marginalised, stigmatised and terrorised a significant section of humanity. The hurt, anguish and indignation faced by transgenders, overweight people, atheists and non-conformists in highly religious and structured societies are indicative of the huge problems the idea of normal can create in our lives.

It is understandable that the idea of normal will have to be used in certain fields, such as mathematics, technology and medicine, but it cannot be used in the social field to judge human conduct. Perhaps instead of asking whether something is normal, it makes sense to ask if something is right, if there is love and compassion in our approach to the world, if what we believe in and practice is conducive to everyone's well-being. It's time to discard outdated ideas of normality and embrace the multiple ways of being and doing things. We do not know the many mysterious ways of life. Let's accept that and let all flowers in nature to bloom to their full potential.

What is Happiness?

Voluminous literature has been composed on the subject of happiness for centuries now; it has been a perennial concern of human beings. There is hardly a philosopher, theologian or psychologist who has not sought to define and explain it in their work. It is generally agreed upon that the experience of joy, contentment or deep satisfaction, combined with a sense that one's life is good, meaningful and worthwhile, constitute happiness.

But imagine the following scenes:

> A Hindu mob lynches a Muslim who is transporting beef, a Muslim terrorist blows up a truck carrying

> Indian soldiers, a student passes his exams with good marks, a political candidate wins an election with a huge margin, a Christian monk wins over the hearts of a hundred tribal people and converts them to his faith, a young man succeeds in overcoming all obstacles and marries his girlfriend, a poor man wins a lottery worth ten crores. Wouldn't they all dance with joy and feel that their lives are good and meaningful?

Would we call the scenes above as happy? How else would you describe them? As jubilation, pleasure or self-satisfaction? Perhaps many would object to the act of killing as one inducing happiness and maintain that it is wrong. A genuine sense of happiness, a philosopher might argue, must be one with a basis in morality. A biochemist would most likely disagree and explain that when a person does or supports something they like, happy hormones such as serotonin, dopamine or oxytocin kick in, causing pleasure and happiness. While the death of someone from another religion might make one person happy, another could find joy in something more ethical.

If so, then we need to ask: is happiness a state of mind, or is it a result of something we do? We experience a sense of fullness and joy that the world is a wonderful place when we do what we like or get what we desire. On the other hand, when that doesn't happen, we get frustrated and sink into despair.

It is a fact that some people are easily disposed to happiness while others need a lot more to feel joy. For some, even little things, say, a piece of cake would make them happy, while there are those for whom getting even a large chunk of the cake is not good enough, and there is no guarantee that they would be happy even if the whole cake is offered to them. This is called greed. Those who are less greedy may have a greater capacity for happiness, while those who are too demanding might never taste happiness at all.

Today, given the rising consumerism, there is a peculiar situation created by the market forces that manufacture limitless desires. So it has become difficult to define and distinguish between needs and wants.

Once the basic needs of food, water, clothing and shelter are fulfilled (though a considerable portion of the human population lack even that), we seek things to satisfy our psychological needs. This often translates into tempting desires, reaping, in the process, both pleasure and pain. It is, to use the popular term from Indian philosophy, the beginning of samsara, which means to toil. We work hard to be happy but the journey brings in sorrow as well. Sadly, pain and pleasure always come together. It seems perennial happiness is not possible; perhaps there is no such thing. If that is so, is it possible to opt for one and reject the other? I don't think so. Joy and sorrow, laughter and tears follow each other, just like the tail follows the monkey; they are an inescapable part of the human condition.

It appears that the very search for happiness is the problem. So long as we are seeking happiness, disappointment, sadness, anxiety and fear are bound to follow. So one might argue that the desire for happiness, perennial happiness in particular, is an illusion. Following this reasoning, we might say that if one abandons the search for permanent happiness, then sorrow would end too. What then should we do? Joseph Campbell would say: 'Follow your bliss.' By that he means: do the right thing, pursue what is close to your heart or what you love. His suggestion implies that shedding all ideas that cause conflict, and working for excellence and wholeness, would be a wise way of living.

Having said that, it is necessary to distinguish between happiness and pleasure, which are often used as synonyms. Philosophers have pointed out that the pursuit of pleasure and avoidance of pain is the factor that drives the functioning of human beings. In fact, most human activity is born out of sensuality. Eating, bathing, smoking, troubling people one dislikes, buying things one likes, listening to music and having sex are all activities that give us pleasure. Thought turns these sensory experiences into a pleasure movement which seeks repetition. For instance, sexual activity, which is biological in nature, is something we turn to again and again because it gives us pleasure. It has become possible for humans, as opposed to animals, to have sex at any time they want through the help of thought.

It is said when dopamine is released in the brain, one feels temporary pleasure, while serotonin produces a sense of happiness, calmness or well-being that may last for a while.

Simple pleasures are an essential part of a good life, without which living can become dull. However, the fact remains that there is no pleasure without pain. Pleasure is short-lived, hence the urge for its repetition, which then becomes a habit. One wants it more and more in regular doses, without which one feels sad and depressed. There is no *trupti*, a sense of contentment.

It is here that the consumer industry steps in. It works not by fulfilling the genuine needs of people but by catering to their insatiable desires. In the process, they create newer, almost endless wants that can never be fulfilled. They work on the weakness and vulnerability of the human psyche.

In contrast to the pleasure movement that requires constant repetition, happiness may be seen as satisfaction experienced in the inner recesses of one's being. It is not something you need to purchase or work hard to attain. A beautiful sunset, cool breeze, the smile of a child can make one happy. The feeling might be triggered by external factors but it does not entirely depend on them. This kind of happiness is not the opposite of pain. It is beyond pleasure and pain; it is a sensation of inner calmness. It is neither complacency nor the absence of desire, but an ability to be at peace with oneself.

Maslow, the American psychologist, analysed happiness in terms of fulfilment of a hierarchy of needs, such as basic needs, social desires and an ultimate spiritual urge to become whole. He theorised that the need for happiness does not necessarily stem from lack, but from an urge to grow as a person and fully realise one's inner potential. It falls in line with Campbell's suggestion to 'follow your bliss'—pursue what you love most.

Pleasure is a conscious experience. You know that you are having fun and it is going to be short-lived. So you'll have to come back to it to feel that way again. When you can't, the memory of it can be painful because you may think your life is not good enough. By contrast, happiness is an unconscious experience. You cannot look for or chase it like pleasure, for it will be like chasing the horizon. But when you live a life that's closer to your heart, happiness in the form of calmness, peace and contentment will come naturally, like a gentle sea breeze.

Why Do Bad Things Happen Only to Me?

In the life story of the Buddha, you may have heard the famous tale of Kisa Gotami and the mustard seed. The story goes that after losing her only son, Kisa sank into unbearable grief. Taking pity on her, an old woman advised her to seek the Buddha's help. Since he was an enlightened master with miraculous powers, he could help her, she said. Kisa went to the Buddha and pleaded with him to help bring her son back to life. The Buddha told her that he would help her if she could get mustard seeds from a family where no one had died. Kisa ran to her village, desperate to get the seeds, but she could not find a single house that had not suffered the death of a family member. Soon, she realised that death had spared none. Impermanence was the law of life. She buried her son in the forest and let go of her suffering.

Kisa's story is about how nothing lasts forever, and how death is not an end but a part of life. Yet, it is not easy to stop asking questions like, 'Why me? Why should I get cancer, lose my companion, suffer the loss of my child, when the whole world seemed to be enjoying uninterrupted happiness? Why should I suffer alone?'

We need to understand that suffering touches everyone in some form or another. We just don't see it while we are immersed in our own sorrow. Joy and sadness are a part of everyone's lives. We are all affected by the vicissitudes of life. The Buddha is believed to have died from food poisoning; Jesus bled to death on the cross; Ramana was killed by cancer, so were many saints, sages and scientists. Death lays its icy hand on everyone; it doesn't discriminate, be it a saint or a thief, a king or a beggar. What matters is how you accept death.

Once, while talking about his withering body, Ramakrishna is believed to have said, 'This is but a perforated drum, and if you beat it day and night, how long will it last?' Ramakrishna's body, too, was naturally subject to the laws of nature, so it is futile to ascribe some mystical reason to the illness and death of saints and sages.

However cruel it may sound, suffering is an intense egocentric experience. It makes your sense of separateness from others acute and unbridgeable. Some people withdraw from the world and lose interest in life, some plunge into a hectic activity to forget their pain, some wallow in despair and complain about everyone and everything and some people even commit suicide. The major cause for this kind of suffering is our culture which has conditioned us to think of everything that happens in our lives on purely personal terms. The suffering becomes so intense and unbearable that we either desperately try to escape it or succumb to it.

It would help us to accept that all our thoughts, feelings and experiences are fleeting. But the egoic mind pulls them back, especially experiences of sadness, and refuses to let them go. The egoic mind is used to thinking that suffering belongs to it alone. So the mind gives it life and strengthens it, resulting in further pain. And when the pain becomes too much, when the body–mind cannot take it any longer, we collapse. But when we let go of the pain, it moves away, becomes toothless and cannot bite you anymore.

Suffering can also trigger in us a desire to know what life is all about. When we question our suffering, we also question our experiences, ideas and beliefs. And we are finally able to see how they are all related and depend on each other for their continuity, and how they produce joy as well as suffering.

Are There Positive and Negative Ways of Thinking and Living?

Self-help books are extremely popular these days. They tell readers how to overcome fears and anxieties, beat lethargy and distress, manage anger and rise above depression, develop healthy pride and confidence and think and act positively to lead a life of joy and contentment.

Perhaps we need to pause here and ask ourselves: why have these self-help books become so hugely popular? Why are psychotherapists, counsellors and gurus in such great demand? Is it because we are increasingly becoming a society of sick people, endlessly troubled by our fears and prone to despondency? If so, have these books and gurus really helped us? Whatever happened to the great religions who promised salvation and heavenly bliss, and political revolutions who assured us justice and freedom? Did something go wrong, did we get on a wrong ship and end up in the wrong place?

These are not cynical questions. And I am not saying that nothing good has happened in the world, or that all human effort over the centuries has gone to waste. I ask these questions to highlight the fact that despite all the progress we have made in different fields, the human condition hasn't changed much. Human greed and misery, conflicts and our propensity to destroy, kill and control have remained the same. The so-called philosophy of positive thinking operates at a superficial level, without ever coming to terms with the deeper aspects of the human psyche that shape and drive human lives.

Life cannot be thought of in terms of binaries. Concepts of good and evil or sin and redemption have wreaked havoc on our lives. In the name of justice, god and salvation, we have perpetrated untold crimes.

Human emotions, too, are seen in binary terms. Cheerfulness, enthusiasm, optimism, joy and confidence are seen as positive emotions, while sadness, fear, anger and distress are considered negative. We use these labels to describe the different state of our body–mind at a given moment, and this prevents us from looking inwards to understand the play of energy in us.

It is important, therefore, to know why we are sad, jealous, angry, lethargic, fearful, depressed or hopeless, instead of rushing to become cheerful, courageous, confident and hopeful just because some book or guru said that these emotions are bad.

The so-called negative emotions are windows of opportunities to understand ourselves. We might be jealous of somebody's success because we suffer from low self-esteem. We are frustrated because our plans for the future have been thwarted. We feel depressed because there is loss of a sense of direction or because the future seems bleak due to an unexpected occurrence. Understanding this honestly can be liberating because then we can learn to deal with these challenges creatively instead of sidestepping them to develop so-called positive emotions.

It is bad counselling to teach people to reject their so-called negative emotions. Resentment, anger, fear, distress and hatred are all realities of human living and to advise people to discard them is to teach people to indulge in self-denial. This is never going to be helpful. Instead, we need to learn to accept all emotions, how they impact our lives and what can be done about them, especially since they drain our energy and make us miserable.

It is not enough to say, 'I am joy' or 'Everything is beautiful.' You should also accept that the anger that poured out of you, the hatred you expressed, the stab of jealousy you felt are all part of you. Accepting these emotions does not mean you nurture hatred, or let fear and anger grow within you, or go about abusing people or commit suicide. It means you acknowledge that you are made of these multiple selves. This is similar to going to a medical doctor and describing your illness without reservations, without judgement, which makes you feel lighter, better and ready to tackle the disease head on.

Once you embrace yourself fully, you will see how certain emotions like hatred and malice damage you and your relationships, how they drain your energy and why they are not conducive to healthy, intelligent living. And you will work to rise above them.

There are no positive and negative ways of living. There is only living (which is always a mixed bag). There is a right way to do it, and our job is to find out what works for us. Books and gurus might help to an extent, but ultimately only we can free ourselves from suffering. No one can save us but ourselves. We need to learn to be *self-reliant*, take responsibility for our behaviour, be completely honest with ourselves. And then the right action will follow naturally.

Is Anger Bad or Good?

There is a story of an extraordinary woman, who was the wife of a famous writer and a cultural icon. Let's call her S. The story of S could be that of millions of women and men.

S lost her mother when she was only eight years old. Her father married again and her stepmother resented the presence of S and her two younger sisters. Even at that young age, S became protective of her sisters and took care of them. S was an extraordinarily intelligent and lively girl. She excelled in studies and grew to be a good singer and musician. At eighteen, she fell in love with a budding writer and a gifted artist.

Going by the writings of S's husband and the accounts of her children, who were accomplished professionals in their respective fields, you get a picture of a woman who was god-like. She was kind and selfless, took great care of her children and supported her genius husband by sacrificing her own urge to excel in the field of literature and music. She even took care of the orphans for whom her husband started a school. S also entertained and cooked for guests and friends who came to visit the famous artist. She never complained or showed her irritation.

In her forties, she was struck by depression. The sparkle in her eyes went away and the warmth in her heart turned cold. The extreme mood swings made her cantankerous, brash and abusive. It seemed the goddess had turned into a demon overnight. S's husband was understanding but had no time for her. The children who were now pursuing their own careers didn't have much time for her either. She lived on medication and died in her early sixties.

This is a sad story. S never addressed the probable trauma she suffered when her mother died, and the relentless stress under which she lived as a young girl, wife and mother. Did the unresolved trauma, unfulfilled desire and unexpressed anger cause her depression? Why did she shout at people, especially her husband, when she grew older? If S had tried to express her own desires and fulfilled them, if she had given vent to her frustrations and any other psychological stress she was going through, could it have prevented her from falling into depression?

As Gabor Mate, in *The Myth of Normal*, writes, 'Both anger suppressed and anger amplified out of proportion are toxic.' While suppressed anger can undermine self-growth and fulfillment, lead to health issues and result in anxiety and depression; amplified anger can disrupt relationships, cause self-harm and result in destructive consequences. So, without idealising or exaggerating the significance of anger, let us understand that it is often a sudden burst of energy and that subsides just as quickly once its task is completed, which could be an expression of resentment or dissent against something that is unjust. It often has a transformative effect. We can also get angry to protect our physical and emotional boundaries, a trait we seem to have inherited from animals. Animals express anger when they sense danger; it's a protective mechanism.

With human beings, anger takes on a moral dimension as well. At this point, it is crucial to distinguish anger from frustration. What is generally referred to as anger is often annoyance that dissolves into abuse, ranting and even violence. We get upset or annoyed when our expectations or wishes aren't met. Frustration is an exhausting experience, while anger is energising and empowering. However, it is not always easy to distinguish between the two because frustration can masquerade as righteous anger, especially when it takes on different ideological shades and seeks justification.

The story of Jesus' anger can serve as an interesting metaphor here. All four canonical gospels of the New

Testament recount the story of Jesus visiting the Temple of Jerusalem, where he finds merchants overrunning the temple and dealing in unethical trade. Jesus reprimands them and drives them out, saying, 'My house shall be called the house of prayer; but you have made it a den of thieves' (Mathew 21:12–13).

The story of Jesus driving the money changers away became a source of inspiration for the development of 'liberation theology' in the late nineteenth century Latin America, which then spread all over the world. Jesus' stand against unethical traders was seen as an example of righteous anger and interpreted as a dynamic call against all forms of oppression and injustice.

This indeed is an inspiring tale as it reveals the liberating effect of anger but, we need to pause here and understand that unless it embodies non-violent ethics, it can take on aggressive, destructive forms and turn antithetical to the teachings of Jesus, one of the greatest apostles of love and non-violence. Having said that, it is worth repeating that it is of critical importance to distinguish between anger and frustration—anger can be a good thing, a noble, virtuous emotion, if used with caution and wisdom.

Are Non-violent Ethics Possible?

For many, 'non-violence' isn't a pleasant-sounding word like 'love', even though in its positive sense, non-violence is love. Throughout history, we have seen how in the name god, religion, politics and family, people have not hesitated to destroy and kill. One may, of course, argue that that is not true love. However, it is almost impossible to kill in the name of non-violence.

Not many people are convinced about the relevance of non-violent ethics and they would most likely point out that we live in violent times and we cannot, like Jesus taught, turn the other cheek to our aggressor. And for all you know, he may slap you harder than before. Someone else might argue that even Gandhian non-violence has become irrelevant today; in fact, even during his time, he couldn't have succeeded in his non-violent struggle against, say, Adolf Hitler and his fascist regime. That the British put up with satyagraha because they could not go against the judicial system they themselves had created.

It is true that we share a lot of traits with animals. The propensity for aggression and violence is a major one. Yet, we have to admit that humans are more violent than animals. Yet, for ages now we have been misled into thinking that animals are innately brutal. Long years of ethological studies have revealed that animals are certainly not as violent as we thought them to be, and absolutely not as brutal as humans have been.

In well-documented field studies of animals, including chimpanzees, tigers and grizzly bears, it has been found that many species of animals are more peaceful, cooperative, empathic and compassionate than previously believed. Animals' behaviour has a biological basis. Humans share this trait with the animal world. However, thought has complicated human life and seems to have taken over instinct, making us more aggressive than animals.

We inflict pain on others and even go to war not because we are naturally driven to do so, or that it is a survival instinct. Rather, we are culturally and ideologically-driven. It is ironical that, on the one hand, if egalitarian values and values embedded in empathy and compassion make us noble animals, on the other, ideologies, whether religious or political, that approve of violence and the elimination of those who do not fall in line with us, make us worse than animals.

However, our redeeming feature is that across cultures, despite the violent beliefs, most of us are actually kind, generous and empathetic. This gives us hope that building a mature society based on non-violent ethics is possible. The knowledge that humans can also eschew violence is heartening.

We know with absolute certainty that humans will never willingly live under the rule of one law, god or religion. Political differences will always exist because of cultural and linguistic divides. These differences are a wonderful aspect of human living. People understand the truth both subliminally and intellectually that there will always be disagreements. From there rises the need to cooperate and coexist, to resolve disputes through non-violent means. Empirical data shows us that attempts to resolve disputes non-violently have often been more effective than armed struggles.

Dr Gene Sharp, in his various books and publications on non-violent struggles, has effectively argued that from the late eighteenth century to the twentieth century, peaceful methods were widely used in colonial rebellions, international political and economic conflicts, religious conflicts and anti-slavery resistance with a high success rate. Sharp has identified nearly two hundred large-scale non-violent struggles to date. The methods included protest marches, rallies, picketing, social and economic boycotts, strikes by workers and civil servants, civil disobedience, boycott of rigged elections, hunger strikes, establishment of alternative institutions and many more.

Ordinary people from all walks of life participated in them. They may not necessarily be pacifists, but they are aware that non-violent actions to resolve conflicts are a more creative and constructive option.

As Sharp would argue, it is incorrect to believe that violence is more effective. History shows us that resorting to violent means have had dangerous political consequences and caused immense suffering. On the contrary, non-violent methods have brought victories quickly, sometimes within days or weeks. As Sharp says, 'The view that nonviolent struggle is impossible except under rare conditions is contrary to the facts. That which has happened in the past is possible in the future.'

It is a cleansing fact that throughout history, marginalised people, especially women, have waged non-violent, silent battles against injustices, and have also nurtured humanity. Yet we seldom acknowledge, let alone commend, their sacrifices and peaceful resistance. So, let us not ask whether it is possible to 'turn the other cheek', whether non-violent ethics are relevant for our times. It is possible, and it is a lived experience, not some irrelevant ideal or a utopian future. It makes more sense to ask how and why we need to build on what has been a vital part of our very being, which alone can sustain and nurture life on our planet.

Is Rebirth Possible?

This is a tricky question and the answer is both yes and no. Broadly speaking, rebirth is possible because, in a sense, it is a continuous process in nature. Things die and then are reborn.

So birth and death and rebirth are a fact of life. Perhaps there is no complete destruction of any being. And from the residue, life emerges again. But what is reborn is not the same thing that died. It is a completely new being. Hence, we can say that there is no death and no birth, only what may be cautiously called evolution and involution. In that sense, life is eternal.

I think everyone understands this aspect of life and nature. What someone means by rebirth is: will, say, Z be reborn after death? Will I be reborn? Will my daughter/son/wife/husband who died so young come back to life?

The questions that follow immediately are: What *is* reborn? Is it the self, the 'I' with all its memories, its desires and fears? Or is it the soul which is supposed to be untouched by samsara and is immortal?

Garuda Purana, composed around 900 CE, has sermons and discourses about cosmology and different philosophies, about karma and rebirth, hell and funeral rites, liberation from the rebirth cycle and so on. The text goes into details of how, after death, the soul gets disconnected from the body and why it hovers over familiar places and people for seven days. It happens because of unfinished business, excessive grief, guilt or fear of moving on to the astral plane. The delay in entry to the astral plane could also happen, the text explains, because of improper last rites. Rituals have to be conducted properly within twelve days of death to enable the soul's journey to heaven or hell, depending on its karma. While this has created fear and confusion in the minds of people, it has also allowed the priestly class to step in with their expertise in eschatology.

The *Garuda Purana* is certainly a highly imaginative work, put together by very clever people. But we are told that it is a dialogue between Lord Vishnu and his vehicle, Garuda, about death and the afterlife. This is an old trick indulged in by almost all religious texts to claim authenticity and authority, and gain universal acceptance. The *Purana* reads like a fantasy. Lately, it has gained a scientific status. Stories of people remembering their past lives are cited to justify the theory of reincarnation. If their stories are even partly true, then we do not know how these people accessed the memories of the past and if it is actually their experience. As you can see, it is all tied up in knots. Whatever arguments one may offer, it still does not prove 'rebirth' because it cannot be verified with actual evidence. The power of belief, of thought, is such that it can make things appear true. It is perfectly possible that people selectively marshal facts to establish their position.

But let us look at the subject more deeply.

The belief that the soul escapes the body after death and then, after a certain period of time, takes a new body and is reborn on earth, when examined carefully, is riddled with contradictions.

If the soul, according to the many religious texts, especially the *Bhagavad Gita*, is 'unborn, eternal, permanent and ancient', then the soul cannot be spoken about in terms of cycles of births and deaths. For, if we accept a changing soul, then there can be no valid argument for its immutable nature.

Now, let's say that it is not the soul but the ego or the self that is reborn. That belief has no basis either because, as per the many Hindu and Buddhist spiritual traditions:

- if the self is an illusion because thoughts do not belong to you the way, say, your eyes and nose and mouth do,

- if the individual per se does not exist. Rather, there are only thoughts. And the self or the 'I' emerges by way of identifying itself (selectively) with thoughts, which are a mix of the thoughts of others and of society,
- if it is like picking a few from the seven basic colours found in nature and making a combination of our own,
- then, *who* or *what is reborn*?

Indeed, what exactly is reborn? By studying spiritual texts that dwell on the nature of body, mind and consciousness, and what sages have said about the subject, what is reborn is the thought structure and its different shades, which is the cumulative result of human thinking over millions of years. The thought structure always continues. It is like a tree putting out a seed that produces another one like it. The new one is not the same tree but has all the characteristics of the mother tree. So, just as it is in the nature of a tree to reproduce one like itself, so is the nature of thought. That is rebirth, the perpetuation of samsara, thought structure, the bhavachakra or the wheel of existence. So it's not Z who will be reborn, but the thought structure. This process does not happen after death or at the end of one's life. It is happening right now, at every instant and with every breath as you read these words.

What Is Sacred and Divine?

Many things are considered sacred. Any object or place associated with religious, spiritual, divine persons are thought of as holy.

You may, of course, rightfully ask: When something is called 'sacred', it implies that something else is not divine.

Does that even make sense? If god is the cause and source of all existence, how can a particular place, book, person, music or thought be considered divine? Why shouldn't we consider every form of life, including every human being, divine? Why do we attribute the quality of divinity only to certain persons, objects and places? Isn't the farmer who grows our food, the sweeper who cleans our streets, the cobbler who makes sandals, the woman who gives birth divine? Doesn't every thought we have, every word we utter, any action we perform, every musical note we play come from the same source, god or nature?

We use words like 'sacred' or 'holy' for certain groups to privilege them over others. This is a cultural invention without any basis in divinity. This need to create a hierarchy of values has been the cause of all conflicts around the world.

The sacred versus the materialistic is just like any other binary, such as beautiful and ugly, good and evil. Such binaries have succeeded in only creating fake values and false consciousness. Nothing high or low, evil or good. Everything emerges from the same source and everything is divine and sacred.

You may still argue that identifying and naming certain emotions such as pride, greed, lust, envy and wrath as evil would help us create a better world. But has that happened? I don't think so. This approach has not helped people overcome their greed, nor prevented rape or violence. Belief in the idea of the divine has not made the humans better; in fact, it has become only easier to hate and kill in the name of the divine. It would thus be wise to ask not what is divine but what is right and life-affirming? Is the action rooted in empathy and compassion? Will it reduce suffering, and promote harmony and well-being?

There is another argument in favour of the idea of the sacred. Places of worship, like temples and mosques, and places of the birth of religious/spiritual masters, including where their bodies are interred, are holy shrines because they are centres of great positive forces. It is said that these places transform lives of devotees for good. Some also believe that miracles happen there—people's problems are solved, their diseases cured—strengthening their faith and steering them towards god.

The question is: Does that really happen? If it does, we need to ask why many such sacred places have become centres of wealth and exploitation, and why they haven't succeeded in solving the ills that plague the world.

I am not, of course, criticising belief in the divine. I neither approve nor disapprove it, and definitely do not dismiss the subject. But we are critically examining the notions of the sacred, not so much from the rational framework as from a life-affirming, spiritual perspective that inspires people to consider every form of life as holy. If you are a true believer, isn't that what a good god expects of you?

The bhakti movement, which started in the sixth century CE and spanned several centuries across the Indian subcontinent, was about a quest for the divine, not in the so-called sacred places or texts but in everyday activities and living and in every atom of creation. In part, it was also a rebellion against the dominant Brahminical ideology that had appropriated the belief in the god into its structure of hierarchical practices. Women and people belonging to the lower castes challenged the central religious narratives by rejecting the spiritual authority of the Vedas and oppressive features of Brahminical tradition. In contrast to *anubhava*, or experiencing the divine through the mediation of priests or clerics and texts, *anubhaava* was an earnest call for unmediated, direct vision of the divine. Allama Prabhu, Akka Mahadevi, Basavanna, Ravidas, Lalleshwari and Kabir, to name a few, were at the forefront of this vital, cleansing stream within the bhakti movement.

For that matter, even before the bhakti movement, saints, mystics and sages had repeatedly pointed out the absurdity of clinging to rituals, the dangers of spiritual authority and the institutionalisation of god. Religions may make you believe in god, holy places and symbols, but they seldom enable a direct experience of the divine. In fact, they take you away from god, that great vibrant presence which is all-pervasive beyond name and form. True devotion needs no mediation because all the mediating agents—temples and priests, mosques and mullahs—more often than not block your spiritual growth, condition you to depend on their authority and parochial discourses, and put you on a long winding path that hardly ever leads you to directly experience the divine.

Among the sages and mystic-poets, Kabir's was a radical and refreshing voice—at once a critique of the tyranny of organised religions and a call to return to the unmediated vision or experience of that which has no name or form.

O servant, where dost thou seek Me?
Lo! I am beside thee.

I am neither in temple nor in mosque:
I am neither in Kaaba nor in Kailash:
Neither am I in rites and ceremonies,
nor in Yoga and renunciation.
If thou art a true seeker, thou shalt at once see Me:
thou shalt meet Me in a moment of time.
Kabir says, 'O Sadhu! God is the breath of all breath.'
(Shah, trans., 1977)

Centuries before Kabir, in twelfth-century Karnataka, Basavanna, a mystic-poet and social reformer, rebelled against the authority of the Vedas, the caste system and the priestly class. The vibrant spiritual movement he started rejected Brahmanical notions of caste purity and pollution; encouraged widow remarriages; and departed from fire worship and the Vedic rituals related to birth, marriage and death. To these revolutionary measures, Basavanna added a firm renunciation of temple worship, since they had become centres of wealth and corruption. Instead, he developed a spirituality of liberation that was congenial to the common man.

The rich will make temples for Shiva.
What shall I, a poor man, do?
My legs are pillars, the body the shrine,
the head a cupola of gold.
Listen, O Kudalasangamadeva,
things standing shall fall,
but the moving ever shall stay.

This *vachana* of Basavanna powerfully summarised the central concern of the new radical cult of Shiva he founded. In A.K. Ramanujan's words, the temple is a 'static standing thing that has forgotten its moving originals' and Basavanna's poem 'calls for a return to the original of all temples, preferring the body to the embodiment'.

Almost a hundred years before Basavanna, Devara Dasimayya, a weaver who had inspired Basavanna's spiritual insurgency, criticised the caste system, gender discrimination and the beliefs and practices that were narrow, hierarchical and binary in their outlook. In one of his powerful vachanas, he said that for a Shiva devotee, things like auspicious time and place do not exist. If at all, their *front yard* can be the holy site of worship.

Epilogue

We have seen how binary notions have permeated our lives, why they have not worked and are unlikely to do so in the future. Yet we stubbornly cling to what needs to be cast aside.

We are afraid to let go of things and ask ourselves if it is indeed possible to live without beliefs that have come to us from religions and political discourses. We wonder what our identity will be if we discard our beliefs, much like a man losing all his money and becoming a pauper. This book has been an attempt to tell you that once the heavy baggage of ideas is discarded, you are likely to become free, light and cheerful. There is no ultimate goal to reach because it doesn't exist. Living itself is the goal. We should all live fully and honestly with the awareness that we are part of the mystery that is life and go with its flow.

The painful yet blessed fact is that we have never been able to live up to our belief system. If we had, the world would have been a crazier, more terrible place. If we have been able to live with some peace, harmony and happiness, it is because we have not fully followed these grand ideas. It could be our innate intelligence that has saved us from destroying each other.

But I wonder how long we can last without breaking free from ideas that divide life into irreconcilable binaries. By giving up these divisive notions, we lose nothing except the chains that bind us to them which make our lives miserable. We need to give ourselves a chance to be free of all these dogmas.

There was a time when all train passengers were instructed to travel light by not carrying unnecessary luggage. It was good advice that made our journey comfortable. It can be implemented in the journey of life too. It is smart policy to shed the baggage of beliefs we have been carrying, which will enable us to see things more clearly, think more lucidly and live wisely.

The idea of truth is the heaviest and the most mischievous. Our many notions of what is true invariably convert our life into a battlefield. The inherent logic is that there can be only one version of the truth, and everyone has to believe it without asking any questions.

Any claim to a notion of truth invariably leads to exclusiveness, which results in intolerance and contempt for those who do not fall in line. For instance, a person who follows one religion or ideology strictly would inevitably call the truths of other religions false and, therefore, 'other' needs would have to be converted or crushed. The idea of truth as absolute, infallible and exclusive would mean perpetual war unless truth embodies a steadfast faith in non-violence and compassion.

The other (perhaps more creative and intelligent) way would be to humbly accept that we do not know the absolute truth. What we have are only certain views about what is true. Truth cannot be captured in any conceptual framework. Most conflicts are rooted in conditioned mental bias. For instance, when Indians and Pakistanis, or Arabs and Israelis look at the world with a certain fixed idea of reality, they will all invariably assert those instances that prove them to be right. They are unwilling to concede that what they see through the lens of their ideology is only their point of view—and not the truth.

Thus, what we have are only socially constructed, subjective views about truth, reality, god, freedom, development, sovereignty, purpose, death, afterlife and so on. This understanding would have tremendous social, political, cultural and individual implications. Accepting that we cannot see the full picture, and merely have different views about it can create space for dialogue, empathy and inclusiveness, fostering integral growth. It may not be an easy approach since we have been conditioned to think of truth in absolute terms, but it'll certainly be an honest one, for there is no other way out of the present crisis. Uncompromising, fearless honesty is what will cleanse us of false gods and goals and illuminate the path we need to walk on.

Bibliography

Life

1. Rao, Mukunda. *In Search of Shiva: A Novel*. Bangalore: Dronequill Publishers Pvt. Ltd, 2010.
2. Eliade, Mircea. *From Primitives to Zen; A Thematic Sourcebook of the History of Religions*. London: Harper Collins, 1977.
3. Brihadaranyaka Upanishad.
4. Campbell, Joseph. *Oriental Mythology*. London: A Condor Book, Souvenir Press, 2000.
5. Armstrong, Karen. *A History of God*. London: Vintage, 1999.
6. Armstrong, Karen. *Mohammad: Prophet for Our Time*. London: Harper Perennial, 2006.
7. Gray, John. *Straw Dogs—Thoughts on Humans and Other Animals*. London: Granta Books, 2003.
8. Rao, Mukunda. *The Buddha: An Alternative Narrative of His Life and Teaching*. New Delhi: HarperCollins, 2018.

God

1. Armstrong, Karen. *A History of God*. London: Vintage, 1999.
2. Armstrong, Karen. *Fields of Blood: Religion and the History of Violence*. London: The Bodley Head, 2014.
3. Campbell, Joseph. *The Power of Myth*, Joseph Campbell with Bill Moyers. United Kingdom: Anchor Books, 1991.
4. Rao, Mukunda. *The Buddha: An Alternative Narrative of His Life and Teaching*. New Delhi: HarperCollins, 2018.

Religion

1. Huxley, Aldous. *Perennial Philosophy*. New York: Perennial Classics, 2004.
2. Armstrong, Karen. *Fields of Blood: Religion and the History of Violence*. London: The Bodley Head, 2014.
3. Armstrong, Karen. *Mohammad: Prophet for Our Time*. London: Harper Perennial, 2006.
4. Armstrong, Karen. *The Bible: The Biography*. London: Atlantic Books, 2007.
5. *The Koran*, translated with notes by N.J. Dawood. England: Penguin Books, 1981.
6. Daly, Mary. *Gyn-Ecology: The Metaethics of Radical Feminism*. Boston, United States: Beacon Press, 1990.
7. *A Reader in Feminist Knowledge*, edited by Sneja Gunew. London and New York: Routledge, 1991.
8. Rao, Mukunda. *The Other Side of Belief: Interpreting U.G. Krishnamurti*. Gurgaon, Haryana: Penguin Books India, 2005.

9. Rao, Mukunda. *Between the Serpent and the Rope*. Noida, Uttar Pradesh: Harper Collins, 2014.
10. Campbell, Joseph. *The Power of Myth*, Joseph Campbell with Bill Moyers. London: Anchor Books, 1991.

Body, Mind and Soul

1. Rao, Mukunda. *The Other Side of Belief: Interpreting U.G. Krishnamurti*. Gurgaon, Haryana: Penguin Books India, 2005.
2. Arms, Rodney (ed). *The Mystique of Enlightenment—The Unrational Ideas of a Man Called U.G.* Goa: Dinesh Vaghela, 1982.
3. *The Biology of Enlightenment, Unpublished Conversation with U.G. Krishnamurti*, edited with an introduction by Mukunda Rao. New Delhi: Harper Collins, 2011.
4. *The Mind of the Cells—Or Willed Mutation of Our Species*, edited by Satprem. New York: Institute For Evolutionary Research, 1982.
5. Rao, Mukunda. *The Buddha: An Alternative Narrative of His Life and Teaching*. New Delhi: HarperCollins, 2018.
6. Rao, Mukunda. *Sky-Clad: The Extraordinary Life and Times of Akka Mahadevi*. New Delhi: Westland, 2018.
7. Ramachandran, V.S., *The Tell-Tale Brain—Unlocking the Mystery of Human Nature.* Noida, UP: Random House India, 2010.
8. Dharwadkar, Vinay (ed). *The Collected Essays of A.K. Ramanujan*. New Delhi: Oxford University Press, 2001.
9. Davies, Paul. *The Origin of Life*. New York: Penguin Books, 2000.

Knowledge

1. Stevenson, Leslie. *Ten Theories of Human Nature*. New Delhi: Oxford University Press, 1998.
2. Huxley, Aldous. *The Perennial Philosophy: An Interpretation of the Great Mystics, East and West*. New York, HarperCollins, 1990.
3. Popper, Karl. *The Poverty of Historicism, Open Society and Its Enemies*, Vol I & II. New York: Routledge and Kegan Paul, 1977.
4. Dharwadkar, Vinay (ed). *The Collected Essays of A.K. Ramanujan*. New Delhi: Oxford University Press, 2001.
5. Madison, G.B. *The Hermeneutics of Postmodernity—Figures & Themes*. USA: Midland Book Edition, 1990.
6. Capra, Fritjof. *The Hidden Connection*. New York: Flamingo, 2003.
7. Rao, Mukunda. *The Buddha: An Alternative Narrative of His Life and Teaching*. New Delhi: HarperCollins, 2018.

Selfishness

1. Dawkins, Richard. *The Selfish Gene*. New York: Oxford University Press, 1999.
2. Ramachandran, V.S., *The Tell-Tale Brain—Unlocking the Mystery of Human Nature.* Noida, UP: Random House India, 2010.
3. Rao, Mukunda. *The Buddha: An Alternative Narrative of His Life and Teaching*. New Delhi: HarperCollins, 2018.
4. Watson, Lyall. *Beyond Supernature: A New Natural History of the Supernatural*. New York, Bantam Books, 1988.

5. Watson, Lyall. *The Romeo Error: A Matter of Life and Death*. New York: Dell Publishing, 1976.
6. *The Biology of Enlightenment, Unpublished Conversation with U.G. Krishnamurti*, edited with an introduction by Mukunda Rao. New Delhi: HarperCollins, 2011.
7. Mate, Gabor and Daniel Mate. *The Myth of Normal. Trauma, Illness & Healing in a Toxic Culture*. United Kingdom: Penguin Random House, 2022.

Love

1. Sermon on the Mount. The Bible.
2. Gandhi, Rajmohan, *Mohandas: A True Story of a Man, His People and an Empire*. New Delhi: Penguin-Viking, 2006.
3. Rao, Mukunda. *The Buddha: An Alternative Narrative of His Life and Teaching*. New Delhi: HarperCollins, 2018.

Free Will

1. Radhakrishnan, Sarvepalli. *Indian Philosophy*, Volumes I and II. New Delhi: Oxford University Press, 1989.
2. Sangharakshita. *A Survey of Buddhism: Its Doctrines and Methods through the Ages*. London: Tharpa Publications, 1987.

Fear

1. Lawrence, D.H. *Apocalypse*. London: Granda Publishing Limited, 1981.
2. Rao, Mukunda. *The Buddha: An Alternative Narrative of His Life and Teaching*. New Delhi: HarperCollins, 2018.

3. *The Biology of Enlightenment, Unpublished Conversation with U.G. Krishnamurti*, edited with an introduction by Mukunda Rao. New Delhi: HarperCollins, 2011.
4. Wegner D.M. *The Illusion of Conscious Will*. Cambridge, MA: MIT Press, 2002.

Freedom

1. Frost, Robert. *Mending the Wall*. https://www.poetryfoundation.org/poems/44266/mending-wall.
2. Pankaj Mishra. *Age of Anger: A History of the Present*. New Delhi: Juggernaut Books, 2017.
3. Rao, Mukunda. *The Buddha: An Alternative Narrative of His Life and Teaching*. New Delhi: HarperCollins, 2018.

Death

1. Stevenson, Leslie. *Ten Theories of Human Nature*. New Delhi: Oxford University Press, 1998.
2. Hiriyanna, M. *The Essentials of Indian Philosophy*. New Delhi: Motilal Banarsidass, 1995.
3. Rahula, Walpola Sri. *What the Buddha Taught*. Oxford: Oneworld Publications, 2007.
4. Rajagopal, D. (ed). *Commentaries on Living: Third Series, From The Note Books of J. Krishnamurti*. New Delhi: B.I. Publications, 1984.
5. Armstrong, Karen. *Mohammad: Prophet for Our Time*. London: Harper Perennial, 2006.
6. Armstrong, Karen. *The Bible: The Biography*. London: Atlantic Books, 2007.

Maya

1. Rao, Mukunda. *Between the Serpent and the Rope*. Noida, UP: HarperCollins,
2. Rao, Mukunda. *The Buddha: An Alternative Narrative of His Life and Teaching*. New Delhi: HarperCollins, 2018.
3. Arms, Rodney (ed). *The Mystique of Enlightenment—The Unrational Ideas of a Man Called U.G.* Goa: Dinesh Vaghela, 1982.
4. Katz, Steven T. (ed). *Mysticism & Religious Traditions*. New Delhi: Oxford University Press, 1983.
1. Radhakrishnan, Sarvepalli. *Indian Philosophy*, Volumes I and II. New Delhi: Oxford University Press, 1989.

Reflections on Some Frequently Asked Questions

1. Mate, Gabor and Daniel Mate. *The Myth of Normal. Trauma, Illness & Healing in a Toxic Culture*. United Kingdom: Penguin Random House, 2022.
2. Watson, Lyall. *Beyond Supernature: A New Natural History of the Supernatural*. New York: Bantam Books, 1988.
3. Rao, Mukunda. *Sky-Clad: The Extraordinary Life and Times of Akka Mahadevi*. New Delhi: Westland, 2018.
4. Rao, Mukunda. *The Buddha: An Alternative Narrative of His Life and Teaching*. New Delhi: HarperCollins, 2018.
5. Rao, Mukunda. *The Other Side of Belief: Interpreting U.G.* Krishnamurti. Gurgaon, Haryana: Penguin Books India, 2005.

6. Bekoff, Marc. 'Humanlike Violence Is Not Seen in Other Animals—Science Shows that Nonhuman Animals Are Predominantly Nice to One Another', *Psychology Today*, https://www.psychologytoday.com/intl/blog/animal-motions/201212/ humanlike-violence-is-not-seen-in-other-animals.
7. Rao, Mukunda. *India's Greatest Minds: Spiritual Masters, Philosophers, Reformers*. Gurugram: Hachette India, 2022.
8. Sharp, Gene. *Waging Nonviolent Struggles*. Columbia University. See https://ciaotest.cc.columbia.edu/book/ciao.

Epilogue

1. Rao, Mukunda. *The Buddha: An Alternative Narrative of His Life and Teaching*. New Delhi: HarperCollins, 2018.
2. Rao, Mukunda. *The Other Side of Belief: Interpreting U.G.* Krishnamurti. Gurgaon, Haryana: Penguin Books India, 2005.
3. Panikkar, R. *The Intra-Religious Dialogue*. Bangalore: Asian Trading Corporation, 1984.
4. Taleb, Nassim Nicholas. *The Black Swan*. London: Penguin Books, 2008.

Acknowledgements

THE IDEA FOR THE BOOK CAME FROM THE LATE Vivek Phadnis. We were phone friends for over fifteen years. Sadly, he left us before I could meet him with the book. The late Dr Mundra was a loving friend, guide and philosopher, whose home used to be a carnivalesque adda in the evenings for many friends, where spirits and ideas flowed freely. I remember both of these senior friends with immense gratitude.

I am also filled with gratitude to Dr Deependra Moitra and Vidya Ramachandra for reading an early draft of this book and offering their valuable suggestions.

My deep gratitude to the publisher Karthika V.K. for believing in the book, and to Ajitha G.S. for her abiding support.

Last but not least, my grateful thanks to Parita Patel, Sanjana T and Vandana Menon for their brilliant editorial assistance, Saurabh Garge for the wonderful cover and Mukul for his excellent typesetting.